Thank you,
Mary Gail!

The TurnAround Mom

Blessing
to you
&
yours—
Carey

The TurnAround Mom

How an Abuse and Addiction Survivor
Stopped the Toxic Cycle for Her Family
—and How You Can, Too

CAREY SIPP

Foreword by George H. Gallup, Jr., of the Gallup Organization

Health Communications, Inc.
Deerfield Beach, Florida

www.hcibooks.com

Library of Congress Cataloging-in-Publication Data

Sipp, Carey.
    The turnaround mom : how an abuse and addiction survivor stopped the toxic cycle for her family—and how you can, too / Carey Sipp.
      p. cm.
    ISBN-13: 978-7573-0596-2 (trade paper : alk. paper)
    ISBN-10: 0-7573-0596-2 (trade paper : alk. paper)
    Includes bibliographical references.
    1. Alcoholics—Rehabilitation. 2. Alcoholics—Family relationships. 3. Recovering alcoholics—Life skills guides. 4. Self-help techniques. I. Title.

HV5276.S57 2007
616.86'1—dc22   2007001161

Publisher: Health Communications, Inc.
          3201 S.W. 15th Street
          Deerfield Beach, FL 33442-8190

Cover design by Andrea Perrine Brower
Interior design and formatting by Lawna Patterson Oldfield

To Tom, my children, my mother,
and the millions of parents who, in spite of
incredible challenges from the past, are committed
to helping their families create a healthy, positive,
and loving home life—the kind of home life
that helps children thrive.

Contents

Acknowledgments

꧁꧂

Thanks be to God for all the good people who helped me write and produce this book, either through editorial help or by simply believing in me.

Heartfelt thanks in particular to: George H. Gallup, Jr., Valerie Clark, Marie Swirsky, Tigress Entertainment, Nancy Katz-Eder, Jo Howarth, Asa Johnson, Randy and Connie Jones, Jenny Pomeroy, David and Jane Bockel, Caislin Weathers, Barbara Hannah, Sage Mueller, Bob Lancer, Becky White, Becky Short, Kathleen McKinney, Bill Stampler, Barbara Brown Taylor, Sarah Kennedy, Martha Sterne, Phil Schroeder, Betsy Lunz, Byron Leasure, Harry Pritchett, Don Harp, Ron Greer, Keven and Jim Bellows, Felicia Bellows, Dr. Laura Schlessinger, Terry Redman, Pam Brown, Riki Bolster, Linda Wyatt, Mary Radford Wyatt, Whitlow Wyatt, Charlotte Tucker, Mary Wyche and Art Lesesne, Julie and Randy Salisbury, Tom Graf, Mary Yoder, Jody and Eddie Ard, Paula Londe, Mark Bryan, Victoria Hall, Gertha Coffee, Tammy

Joyner, Anne Woodall, Alyson Gondek, Jerry Spicer, Caroline Harkleroad, Marlene Lockwood, Cindy Lou Harrington, Steve Carmichael, Jack Kinney, Ed Taylor, Sarah Bockel, Michael Mossman, Keddy Gonzales, Phil Diaz, Jim Allyn, Ron and Sheilah Fleisher, Anthony Callandrelli, Sis Wenger, Marion Torchia, Stephanie Abbott, Betsy Tice White, Brian Rudolph, Sally, Brenda, John, Virginia, Tom, Steve, MaryAnne, Jimmy, Sherry, Nedra, Mary, Peg, Carolyn, Ruth, Cheryl, Ted, Nora Lee, J.B., Ginger, Janet, Monica, Lucy, Susan, Connie, Sarah, Pam, Jerry, Diane, and Joel.

Thanks to Allison Janse, Carol Rosenberg, and Erin Brown for their help and to the rest of the team at Health Communications.

Also, to my husband, Tom, my children, my former in-laws, my former husband and his wife, and especially my mother, for learning how to find more joy in life. What a gift, Mother, that we've had these healthier, kinder years together. Praise God from whom all blessings flow!

Foreword

The number of homes in America suffering the ravages of alcoholism and alcohol abuse is at a new high according to Gallup surveys going back a half century. Four in ten women (38 percent) now report that drinking has been a problem in their homes.

With alcoholism and alcohol abuse as key components in virtually every major societal problem, one can conclude that America does not have a crime or health problem so much as it has an alcohol problem.

Alcoholism stems, in part, from what Carey Sipp, author of *The TurnAround Mom*, calls "the mother of all addictions"—the addiction to toxic intensity. This addiction, like all the others it generates, is likely to make parents unavailable to their children and is damaging to them in other ways as well. The resulting neglectful and abusive behaviors are most often unintentionally passed on from generation to generation, perpetuating cycles of addiction and abuse.

Toxic Intensity and Alcoholism

Carey tells us that toxic intensity addicts escape reality by creating and maintaining a cycle of chaos, confusion, and anxiety, then seek relief from the negative results through alcohol, other drugs, work, abuse, their own adrenaline, rage, relationships, sex, money mismanagement, overeating, dishonesty, or any other self-destructive, compulsive behavior.

She explains that during the brief period of relief, the addict may take actions—driving under the influence, overspending, overpromising, becoming involved in destructive relationships—that create even more chaos, confusion, and anxiety, thus perpetuating and intensifying the cycle.

Carey asserts that toxic intensity—along with its fellow traveler, alcoholism—is fueled, in part, by our often frantic lives in which we overextend and undercare for ourselves. This self-perpetuating combination creates fear, which fuels intensity and an energy deficit, which in turn clouds judgment.

She believes further that our expectations of what we

need to live "the good life" have moved so far out of line with reality that "we hurt ourselves with addictions and lack of self-care, and hurt others with the resulting irritability, anger, jealousy, violence, and verbal abuse."

Families, Alcohol, and Unavailable Parents

Sadly, many of today's parents simply do not make time to model or teach self-care to their children, much less address alcoholism and other addictions. Nor do they lead their pressured partners or children into even a few minutes of the daily family quiet time this author advocates as a means of establishing or restoring a sane and loving home life. Carey believes that for children, this nonintense family time, along with other gentle practices she advocates, will help prevent the addictions to toxic intensity—and subsequent substances and behaviors—well before the cycle can ever begin.

It is no accident that Carey consistently begins the list of addictions with alcohol. In her case, and in that of many other adult children of alcoholics, the addictions to alcohol and toxic intensity are so intertwined that it is hard to see where one starts and the other ends.

For too many families, alcohol addiction begins—or becomes manifest—when the most vulnerable of family members reaches a most intense and vulnerable time: the teenage years. While an ounce of prevention before teenage drinking begins could save lives and heartache, research shows that many parents are simply not doing a very good job of helping their children learn responsible attitudes regarding the use of alcohol.

At least one-third of teens say they would like to talk about this topic to a greater degree than is presently the case. Yet many parents are not available or interested in talking about attitudes and behavior regarding alcohol, in spite of the horrifying facts: in at least six of every ten child-abuse cases, alcohol is a factor. The number one killer of teens and young adults is highway crashes related to alcohol. Among teens who commit suicide, alcohol is a factor for four of every ten. The same figure applies to adolescent drownings. Yet many parents avoid talking to their teens about these deadly realities.

Nearly half of all teens see drinking as a problem among their peers. The proportion rises to 57 percent among teens age sixteen and seventeen. Although tougher drinking and driving laws have helped reduce alcohol-related driving deaths, twenty-one of every hundred teens report having been in a car at least once with someone their age who was under the influence of alcohol.

When alcohol somehow kills or contributes to the death of a classmate or family member, the pain of grief fuels toxic intensity and anxiety. Yet teens and adults alike are quick to ease their grief, guilt, and anger, ironically, with alcohol.

Our teens have relatively free access to alcohol. About half say it is very easy to buy, and a third say it is fairly easy to buy. Further, many high school students head off to college totally unprepared for a drinking environment, which includes peer pressure–driven binge drinking—consumption of at least five or more alcoholic drinks in one sitting.

Nor are parents serving as very good role models. Nine percent of teens are willing to admit that they drink more alcohol than they should, but a still greater number, 14 percent, say this about their parents.

Why the Lack of Communication?

Why do so many parents fail to keep their children from getting into trouble with alcohol? As Carey theorizes, many parents lead frantic, fast-paced lives and do not make time for this vital topic of discussion. And for parents who drink excessively themselves, fear, embarrassment, and shame probably play a role in their unwillingness to talk about alcohol with their children. These uncomfortable feelings add to the toxic intensity among family members, helping to perpetuate the cycle.

Further, many mothers, because of abandonment, divorce, or choice, lack the help and support of a spouse. Single parenting often leads to fatigue, financial pressures, and children exacting too much freedom from exasperated mothers or fathers—more staple ingredients of toxic intensity and addiction.

Healing and Preventing Addiction— the Role of *The TurnAround Mom*

Many mothers are in denial about their own drinking habits or other compulsive behaviors. Trapped in the disease of addiction, they do not know the liberation that can come through seeking the help of God or a Higher Power and the support of other recovering persons, as are the suggestions practiced in Alcoholics Anonymous, Al-Anon, and other twelve-step programs created by and for those afflicted with addictive behaviors. They do not know that the easiest way to influence their own children to avoid trouble with alcohol and other addictions is to begin, immediately, their own recovery from alcoholism or any other addictive behavior.

Alcoholism and alcohol abuse touch virtually everyone's life in the family or extended family, directly or indirectly. As a recovering alcoholic myself, I am keenly aware of the potential dysfunction that addictions of all sorts, chemical or otherwise, can have upon a home. What is called for, in the case of alcoholism, is not only a cessation of drinking, but a careful examination of the factors behind addiction, and taking the steps needed to deal effectively with these factors. This can often mean a transformation of life not only for the alcoholic/addict, but for the entire family as well. Neutralizing years of addiction and long-held resentments is healing for the parent; what's good for the parent is good for the child.

For anyone trapped in addictions and denial, *The TurnAround Mom* is a precious gift. It is an honest, no-holds-barred account of the author's upbringing in what she describes as a "violent and alcoholic home." It is an accounting of a person willing to neutralize addiction and resentments. It offers the reader one woman's dramatic and encouraging account of how she is coming to terms with her addictions and keeping her life turned toward that which is healing and positive.

The Spiritual Dimension in Recovery

Carey stresses the importance of the spiritual dimension in recovery, and she reminds us that people can be liberated by becoming aware of their problems, accepting them, and taking actions that lead to positive outcomes for themselves and others. She advocates pathways to change, among the most important are turning our lives and our wills over to the care of a power greater than ourselves, which for Carey is God. This means, in part, taking care of ourselves the way a wise father or mother would take care of a child: with love, discipline, understanding, compassion, natural consequences, and forgiveness.

And while she says she truly believes God does for us "what we cannot do for ourselves," she also believes parents modeling sane and sober behavior must always remember that "faith without work is dead," or simply put, "We can't expect our children to walk away from temptations that we cannot walk away from, and we can't expect them to work any harder at controlling tempers, urges, addictions, and compulsive behaviors than we do."

The TurnAround Mom will help break down the wall of denial. It is a book written with sensitivity, love, and humor. In a loving, humble way, Carey's compelling story and practical steps will lead challenged parents onto the fullest road to recovery: healthy self-care, building a support structure, creating a sane and loving home life.

This is a book that deserves to be widely read and will,

I'm certain, help salvage many lives and restore homes to peace and sanity with its basic message: "You've got to raise yourself before you can raise your children."

—*George H. Gallup, Jr.*

Introduction

❦

I believe every mother who has truly looked into the eyes of her child wants a sane, loving home in which to live and rear that child. But for many of us who grew up in the insanity of addiction and abuse, or became addicted, abused, or stretched to the breaking point, there are incredible challenges. Chief among these challenges are the beliefs: If I don't know what it feels like to be sober, calm, and peaceful, if I don't know what an emotionally healthy family life looks like, how can I create a sane and loving home? How can I help my child grow up with balanced emotions? How can I help her recognize and create healthy relationships? How can I teach him to live a life free from *toxic intensity* and compulsive behaviors?

This book is filled with experiences, processes, tips, and tools that I hope answer those questions. The stories within are meant to bring hope—hope that we can see

1

how powerless children are over the situations they're born into, how profoundly they are affected by their parents, and how lives can be changed for the better when there's a willingness to feel and heal past pains, a willingness to grow and learn.

In my volunteer work with women at treatment centers, I often hear stories of women doing what I believe we all do if we are not conscious and committed to a better way: recreating many of the same problems their parents had and seeing their children exposed to situations they swore they'd never put them through.

In our time together we will talk about how difficult it is for those of us with deep emotional wounds to realize, accept, and find gratitude in the fact that we do have choices.

Ultimately, we come to the conclusion that **even if our parents numbed their pain and created even more pain for themselves and others by being alcoholics, addicts, and abusers, we don't have to.** Our parents' pain does not have to be our pain; generations of pain do not have to be passed on to our children.

As I join many far wiser than I who believe "what we

can feel, we can heal," and that "pain we don't heal, we pass on to our children," my hope is that by sharing parts of my journey, you will be guided and inspired to start or continue your own journey to healing. I have seen this happen in the groups I work with. When I read my stories out loud with them, they tell me that they do go back to those similar situations and feel the desperation of their childhoods, the desperation that leads, ultimately, to a resolve to do whatever it takes to make things different for themselves and their children. They say they also feel hope and that they get an idea of how much better life is and will be if they continue in their recovery.

It is such a gift to me to watch tears fuel resolve, and resolve fuel hope and action. What is happening to them as they hear my story is what happened to me as I remembered and wrote it.

My hope is that your reading this book helps you experience the same feelings of sadness, the same feelings of strength and determination, the same feelings of courage and hope. My hope is that going through this process helps us all recognize self-defeating behaviors we use to act out our pain, so we will choose to stop destructive self-sabotage, take responsibility for our actions, and then be still and quiet until reality and reason return. I also hope we learn or affirm how to separate what works from what doesn't, and how to begin or continue the daily routines that create stable, loving lives for our children and ourselves.

I don't have all the answers; this book is for me as much as it is for you. From what I've experienced and what I'm learning from the groups of women I lead, I know that recognizing and dealing with past hurts clears the way for us to feel greater joy today.

If we are to avoid recreating the past, we simply must feel that pain and use it as motivation to make life better for ourselves and our children. Further, it is clear that we must have a source of hope, the hope that comes from being able to visualize what a sane and loving home looks like. That's why it is so important for me to write down and share what my family life is like now that I have experience in recovery. It helps me to remember—and share—that even when things get a little crazy, we do know how to be sane and loving. With God's help, and with some work on our part, we can remember a time when we felt better about each other. Those positive feelings can and will create the shift that pops us up and out of a dark place. That is a turnaround!

I believe parenting, even in the best of circumstances, is a tremendous challenge. As my children get older and the world gets crazier and more violent and the things my family needs to live become more and more expensive, it takes a lot of deep breaths for me to keep my serenity, to keep the turnarounds going. I'm inspired to take those breaths, say my prayers, and keep doing the next right thing, as best I can, because I know the more my children see me deal with my feelings in honest, open ways—instead of using a substance or an abusive behavior to dull or act out the pain—the more likely they are to deal with their losses and disappointments, joys and pains in healthy, mature ways. The more they see me stack one sane and loving action on top of another, the more likely we all are to stay turned toward that which is sane and sober. The more they see me choose sane and loving behavior, the more likely they are to stay the course and do as I do: practice looking for solutions instead of creating more problems.

How This Book Works
Toward Solutions

I've organized this book in a way that helps readers start their own journey toward solutions, their own turnarounds. Each chapter has three vignettes, which, when read in order, are designed to help the reader:

1. Reexperience feelings of being in intense, abusive situations. My hope is that by reading my experiences—which, unfortunately, are not unique—you will feel some of the fear and anger, powerlessness and frustration you felt when you were being abused or active in your addiction, which is self-abuse. I hope you will ultimately have a good cry and decide that, no matter what, you don't want to experience that kind of pain again, and that you don't want your children to suffer it, either.

2. Feel the frustration and anticipation of being a teenager or adult who is still in active addiction and/or abuse, and is ready, or almost ready, to say "enough!"

3. Experience the relief and hope of being in a turn-around state of mind, where we are getting help with abusive situations or addictions and are seeking solutions instead of creating problems.

In putting these recollections together this way, each chapter begins with an essay titled "The Pain Starts Here," then goes to a "History Almost Repeats Itself" piece, and continues with the example called "The TurnAround."

Many of the women at the treatment centers where I volunteer tell me that when I read these vignettes to them, they do go back to childhood memories. Though their experiences are different, the feelings evoked are the same. Fear is fear. Sadness is sadness. Loss is loss. I see their tears; sometimes we cry together. As our time together progresses, the sadness turns into determination, then hope. Ultimately, we feel gratitude and hope at the end of our hour together.

As you read each chapter's three vignettes, perhaps you, too, will move from the fear and sadness shared in the first essay to the anticipation, hope, and joy expressed in the second and third. Perhaps, too, you'll want to read and apply the concluding tips I compiled, created, and continue to use to be a TurnAround Mom. They are the best of the best golden nuggets I've collected over the course of more than a dozen years in recovery. They've served me well; I hope they are a help to you, too.

From Toxic Tornado to TurnAround Mom— The History and the How and Why of My God-Given Turnaround

I thank God every day that I am a mother in recovery.

I grew up in an intense, violent, alcoholic home. My father grew up in intensity and abuse. For a while, I was afraid I would somehow repeat the cycle with my own two children.

Some of us recreate toxic intensity in an attempt to understand, correct, overcome, or be the opposite of it. For those of us with addictions or the combination of addictions and attention deficit disorder (ADD), creating intensity is a form of self-medication—a crisis that makes our bodies produce the adrenaline we "need" to focus and succeed at something, even if the newly "ginned-up" intensity just helps us get out of the trouble we've created.

We also create intensity to divert our attention from what really matters: the sometimes boring option of simply taking care of ourselves and our families. Many of us just go on automatic pilot, living our lives the way our parents did, not realizing that we do have choices. All that being said, please understand this right now: This book is not a condemnation of my parents; today I love them deeply.

My father died of alcoholism and diabetes in 1981, at the age of fifty-six. An abused child himself, I believe he passed along to others the pain he felt at the hand of his father. While I forgive him for acting out his rage and depression, I can't help but wonder how different his life could have been had he been committed to a program of recovery, such as Alcoholics Anonymous, and if he'd had access to modern-day antidepressants.

Today I know his behavior was not my fault. (Many children of alcoholics blame themselves for their parents' behavior.) I believe that sharing what happened and refusing to pass his pain on to my children is my best way of honoring him.

My mother was able to set Daddy's temper flaring in a heartbeat. I know that she put an incredible amount of energy into trying to control his addictions and, in doing so, almost destroyed herself. Though Mother's staying in this violent, alcoholic marriage subjected my brother and me to danger and abuse, I understand how difficult it is to leave an abusive situation when, at times, the situation seems to be improving. Today I am grateful that throughout those hard years, Mother kept on taking us to church, although we sometimes resented it. While we would never dream of talking to anyone about our family secrets, I believe that my youth-group involvement—the routine of going, the friendships, the messages that somebody loved me—probably saved me from wider-scale self-destruction. I am also grateful that in the last few years, Mother and I have both learned that the best way to help an addict is to take great care of yourself, keep the focus on your own issues, and refuse to criticize and react to the addict's behavior. If I start thinking resentful thoughts, I work hard to stay in the present, to look for my part of the problem, and to "let go and let God."

As an adult, I take full responsibility for my actions. I know I must ask for help to face my fears instead of obsessing about them; find healthy ways to deal with problems when I want to numb out with alcohol, food, or work; practice self-discipline and pray for focus and maturity so I can balance my checkbook, pay bills, and fold laundry instead of creating a crisis. (For many years, it was a lot more fun to solve a problem than prevent one.)

I know that my addiction to toxic intensity, or anxiety, is powerful and has been present since I was a child, when I first became hooked on my own adrenaline. Always on full alert for my raging alcoholic father's next screaming, face-slapping, hair-pulling attack on my mother, I used toxic intensity and the extra adrenaline it created to fuel cycles of overwork, exhaustion, sickness, achievement, and failure. When I was fourteen and my parents finally divorced, I started buying things on their charge accounts without their permission—like stealing without stealing. I could get the adrenaline rush and then feel guilty. They could get angry. I could feel sorry for myself and resentful when they blew up at me.

For intensity addicts, guilt, anger, self-pity, and resentment are like mind-altering drugs. A little starts the cycle; a steady supply is never enough.

Like Pearls on a Treasured Necklace: Adding Sane Day After Sane Day

My hope is that by sharing my experiences in this book, we'll have this guide to turn to when we are challenged. We'll have firsthand proof that life does get better. We'll see together that we can be transformed.

We may give up excitement for a steady job, fancy clothes for markdowns at Old Navy or the resale shop, and sacrifice rushing to an important meeting or date in favor of being home for dinner at 6:00 PM every night. But when we ask for help from others, put structure in our lives, and face life on life's terms, God really does "do for us what we cannot do for ourselves." He takes the routine of our days and strings those days together like pearls on a treasured necklace, helping us to turn, one day at a time, our once-hopeless lives into cherished family heirlooms that make a difference, especially for our children. And if we're extremely lucky, our parents are likely to be thrilled by our progress, and to learn from it as well.

When we practice turnarounds, our children grow up in sane environments. We forgive the past and heal generation upon generation of wounds. Parents and children alike grow up together without feeling the need to destroy themselves and one another with alcohol, acting out in anger, drugs, or other high-risk behaviors. A legacy of sanity begins.

Becoming a TurnAround Mom— The One Who Says, "The Insanity Stops Here"

All along my journey to this saner place, I wrote down what was and was not working. I captured thoughts, feelings, and body sensations. I noted ways I acted and ways I chose not to act, and the consequences of my choices. In vivid dreams and gut-wrenching therapy sessions, I

remembered scenes from my childhood and wrote them
down. Some of this may be unsettling to read, but I
believe there are millions of people like I am who've been
exposed to the toxic intensity of growing up in a home
run by addictions and various forms of abuse. We all need
to know that the taint of growing up terrified doesn't have
to last forever. Even without firsthand experience of con-
sistent sanity, we're not doomed to repeat the past.

Many of the childhood snapshots were written while I
was in an almost hypnotic state after being guided
through meditations to visualize, refeel, and then desensitize myself to intense situations. Part of healing comes
in visualizing how I would deal with the situations today
as a strong, capable adult.

I certainly don't believe all of my childhood was
horrible. Parts of it were nurturing: my grandmother
scratching and rubbing my back, my next-door neighbor
letting me talk with her for hours as she cooked, and my
mother, singing or baking when she wasn't totally driven
by her intense co-addiction to my violent and alcoholic
father. I remember that during the reprieves, she would
laugh with us as we imitated opera singers or dug into

the Red Velvet cakes she made for birthdays. Those were important times. Adult children of alcoholics who are exposed to some sanity and love are those most likely to recover.

Yet the overall feeling I associate with my early years is deep, overwhelming fear. There was tremendous negativism, tension, rage, frustration, anxiety, criticism, rebellion, and sheer terror in our home.

The most vivid, real photograph I've seen of my childhood is one of me being held by my mother. I was about a week old. She looked horrified, as though she was about to cry. When I asked her why she looked so sad and afraid in this picture, she finally told me she'd just found out that my father, who had been making moonshine whiskey, had dragged a man behind a horse until the man was almost dead. It was Daddy's way of punishing the man for telling my grandfather about the whiskey making. Somehow Daddy got off without a criminal record or receiving any punishment for his crime.

In a lot of ways, Mother, my brother, and I served time for him. While he drank and the liquor sometimes freed his conscience, we became more trapped in our fears. Fear that we were living with a monster. Fear of what would happen if we left. Or didn't leave.

Seeing what I had seen at home, it's little wonder that even while unconscious I'd hold to the belief that men—even in an effort to save me—were trying to hurt me. When I was eleven years old I fell from a moving vehicle at summer camp and was knocked unconscious. Efforts to save me were traumatic. For many years I feared that memories of and sensitivity to pressure on my face probably had something to do with my father abusing me. I am grateful that a few years ago I recalled and was able to relive parts of that camp accident. I now know that the people who worked to save my life had to put pressure on my face to immobilize my head and neck. Today I believe part of my challenges with attention deficit disorder and some of the associated depression are also the results of that brain injury. I also believe reliving that memory proved that I am never too old to learn and heal. I'm never too old to look for the truth. It's never too late to work toward a solution.

The Payoff

By taking the time to write all of this down, study what I've learned, and keep looking for solutions, I know now that I have a moment-by-moment opportunity to choose toxic intensity or healing. Chaos or structure. Fear or faith.

I can make choices that will either send my little family down the road to a hell on earth, or set us free. Free to be healthy, functional, loving, and sane.

Right this minute it runs a chill up my spine to think I could blow it all with just one drink. Even though the other addictions are powerful, I work hardest to recover from the warped thought processes of alcoholism. The alcoholic attitude that comes over addicts when they drink even one drink is enough to derail the most dedicated parent. Almost as destructive as a drinking binge is the alcoholic's "dry-drunk" state of arrogance and self-righteousness that evokes pomposity or self-pity even without the booze. Not knowing which drink or binge of "dry-drunking" could be the one that fuels the arrogance, pride, and shameless sense of being above consequences is enough to keep me going to recovery-oriented meetings and calling friends to check in about fears, feelings, challenges, successes—any change or "trigger" that could stir the impulse to drink or act out destructively.

Writing this book is further proof to myself of how much my life has changed for the better in the years since I stopped trying to do everything alone, stopped trying to fix it all with alcohol, money, work, and toxic intensity. Again, addicts are loath to ask for help; I have had to ask for lots of help to complete this project!

As I got healthier, I noticed how my setting boundaries and enforcing consequences was having a positive effect on my children, my mother, and others who are important to me. I continued to keep track of saner ways to handle situations, so I could remember and use what I was learning to help my family. As I shared with others what I was learning, it became apparent that my discoveries could be important to them as well.

My Invitation to You to
Become a TurnAround Mom

In "The TurnAround" section of each chapter, I invite you to see the place you come to when *you know you just won't do it the same way anymore—the place where you finally make the commitment to do whatever it takes to create a better, saner, more serene life*. Your commitment begins a miraculous process: you will soon see how you are supported by God, your Higher Power, the universe, life—whatever you want to call it—when your actions are determined by your rock-solid vow to turn toward that which is healthy, and away from that which is destructive.

You are becoming a TurnAround Mom when your actions—what you do, and say, whom you allow into your life, how you choose to spend your time and money, everything—show your children how committed you are to your health, to them, and to your new way of life. That old saying "actions speak louder than words" rings true, too, because your actions attract others into your life who are *being* the same way you are, who have the same values that are important to you. Never was this more evident to me than when, after being a single mom for almost eleven years, my second husband and I were married. He is a kind and generous man whose commitment to his children—and now to my children—is a top priority. At our wedding, which was attended by about 130 friends and family members, my son "gave me away," and my daughter was my maid of honor.

A note of caution: this is not to say everything gets sunny and wonderful once you're committed to a better way of life. But it is amazing how some of the wants that didn't seem to work out—the job that went to someone else, the apartment that got leased ten minutes before I got there, the teacher my child got but really didn't want—turned out to be gifts. These realizations come when I run my life from "the inside out." When I am okay with how I am with myself, I am less affected or afflicted by what the outside world brings. The need to control the environment—people, circumstances, everything—slips away. A peace comes that truly does "pass all understanding." The key is accepting situations and maintaining a commitment to sanity, all the while trusting that I can ask for, and am worthy of receiving, what I truly need.

Understanding my past strengthens my commitment to stop the cycles of addiction and abuse. While I didn't cause what happened in my childhood and certainly couldn't control it, I can forgive it now and learn from it. I commit myself daily to do all that I can to model sanity, sobriety, serenity, forgiveness, responsibility, and self-care to my children. This is how I define "being in recovery" and having "a spiritual awakening." This is how I define what it is to be a TurnAround Mom.

From Entitlement to Gratitude

Before recovery I often acted as though my past entitled me to resent life, live in fear, and escape problems by using any one of a number of intensity-based addictions, especially alcohol, work, procrastination, and money mismanagement.

Now I find the greatest joy in seeking God's will in my life, hearing my daughter sing, watching my son play a game of catch with my sane, sober friends, and helping other parents create sanity and order in their lives. Today, thank God, my mother and I can stay in our "adult selves" 99 percent of the time. We can admit and let go of our mistakes. Our boundaries with each other are strengthening. Strong boundaries make better relationships.

I am grateful to share my story and the "how-to" tools I love most. For me to write or speak this, I have to apply it to my own life and "walk the walk," not just "talk the talk." We are much more likely to stick to our new values and behaviors when we teach those around us the very things we most need to know. To borrow a quote from an unknown author, "To keep what you have, you've got to give it away."

Writing this book does not mean my life is perfect. It is not. I am not. Oftentimes my house is cluttered. My car is dirty and needs a tune-up. My kids—like all children—have their issues. Sometimes I feel irritable, need to put myself into time-out, feel down, get sick, and run late to meetings. I will probably always need help with money management.

This book is about turning myself and my family

toward a saner and more loving home life, not about being perfect. It's not about beating myself to a pulp when I make a mistake, but instead admitting when I am wrong, doing my best to make a correction, and then getting on to the tasks at hand. My choice is to let my children see me choose sanity.

Please allow me to do my own paraphrase of an old saying: Give a parent sanity and love, and you help that parent. Teach a mom or dad how to create a sane and loving home, and you help create a sane family. Teach a family how to help other families, and you can turn around a generation.

A world free of addiction, abuse, and toxic intensity starts with us TurnAround Parents, one mother and one father at a time.

For our children's sake, and our own, let's make the most of this incredible opportunity!

1

Live a Life
of Extreme Self-Care

We treat ourselves the way we want others to treat us.
Our significant others, children, friends, and coworkers
will treat us with respect when we respect ourselves.
Our children learn how to care for themselves by
watching the way we care for ourselves. If we abuse
ourselves—rushing, overeating, drinking, being in toxic
relationships—our children will mirror these behaviors
in their own lack of self-care. If we don't want them to
repeat negative behaviors, we have to stop our own.

THE PAIN STARTS HERE:

Mother is bruised and in a hurry

I am three or four years old, sitting on a cold floor under the table in the kitchen. I have no idea whether it's the middle of the night or early in the morning. I only know that it is dark and that I am under the table watching Daddy hit Mother and push her into the refrigerator. I see their legs go back and forth in front of me. They move a lot. It's scary. I look up. I see him grab her hair and pull her across the kitchen. She hits at him with her broom. He grabs her shirt and it tears. My baby brother cries. I am quiet and can't move. This goes on for a long time. They are loud. She tries to "shhh" Daddy. Daddy gets madder.

Mother is bruised. She has bald places where her hair is pulled out. She cries. She is sad. Very sad. And she is busy. She rushes to put on her makeup. Hurries to pick up the cleaning lady. Drives fast to get the cleaning lady dropped off at our house so she won't be late to the office. Mother is afraid that if she is late to work she will get fired or "talked to" by her boss.

We are rushing for breakfast. To get to church. Choir. School. And I feel sick to my stomach. I throw up at school and don't tell anybody. We rush, and then we wait. Wait for her to pick us up. Or for him to do it. If she's coming, she will be late. If he's coming, it will be scary. I lose either way.

For a while my bed is a safe place. Then I have dreams that my bed is filled with spiders. When I cry about those spiders and try to claw them out of my hair, I wake up Mother and make her mad at me. She lets me sleep in her bed, but every move I make wakes her up and makes her madder and madder.

When I am older I know that Daddy acts this way when he drinks. And that he gets angry very easily. He yells. Cuts furniture. Breaks windows. Threatens with knives and guns. Shoots holes in walls. Shoots a pistol at Mother and me. Throws Mother down the front steps when she is pregnant with my little brother. Hides a

huge, live snake in the toolbox on his truck and then asks
Mother to go get something out of it so she will find the
snake and scream. Pulls a gun on my brother's friend.
Drives fast and drunk with me bouncing around in the
car. The list goes on and on. He is scary. And then he is
sweet. Sad. Sorry. Dressed in a business suit. Looking
normal. Giving us money. Pets. Stuff.

We are all so tired. I am afraid. I do not like living
under the table.

History Almost Repeats Itself:
Hitting Bottom

Bill, my husband of seven years, and I are not happy.
I spend fourteen hours a day downstairs, writing my
brains out on high-pressure advertising assignments,
drinking beer and eating candy bars to calm down or rev
up, depending on the deadline. I make lots of money,
and spend it as fast as I can. I rush to appointments,
choir practice, and whatever else I think I simply cannot
miss. I have been moving at the speed of light like this
for as long as I can remember.

Bill takes on the role of mother. He is caring for the children, cooking, and working on his illustration career on a catch-as-catch-can basis. I am a workaholic, down in the basement, grinding out work, and bringing in money for our family, so we can keep up an image of success that says "Hell, yes, I can do it" to my doubting mother.

I am driven: feeling guilty about not being with the children more and angry with Bill for not being an incredibly successful—read "rich and steadily employed" —illustrator. I am feeling resentful about doing the work, finding joy in doing it well, and feeling empty all at the same time. Obsessed with earning the money, I am not happy until I collect on my invoices, and then spend my earnings in compulsive fits on things I think we "need."

I work with resentment because I begin to feel less and less like a human and more and more like a machine. A sexless, untouched and untouchable, whirring, rabid thing fueled by fear, greed, and anger. And then at other times I feel used, sad, and horribly lonely. I want to howl and scratch and bite. I am my own victim. I have no one to blame but myself, and I hate blame anyway.

I am abusing myself by taking on more and more tight-deadline projects, so I abuse Bill with the cold looks, the effort to control, anger, despair, and rageful spending. It is, to say the least, an intense cycle. I hit deadlines, the ceiling, the bottle, myself. I believe our marriage is broken beyond repair.

By the time our divorce is final, my twitchy, work-addicted state and anxiety have melted me from 125 to 105 pounds. I expand my chaotic life to include a love of fine white wine and an obsessive crush on a younger man who is probably an alcoholic. Thank God he has the sense not to get tangled up with me.

Thank God I've had the sense to hire a babysitter who lives in the basement in exchange for helping me with the children, and that she is a calming force on the children and me.

I have hit a new bottom, and as I read a book about adult children of alcoholics—a book a friend has given to me—I realize I cannot climb out of this alone. And I am not alone. I still have friends. And I have two children and a God-sent babysitter who are counting on me to provide for them. The reality of their reliance on me makes me stop and take a look at my self-destructive behavior. One of my friends tells me to get into a recovery program for alcoholics and their families. I am too worn out to disagree. As I read some of the recovery program literature, I cry and see myself in the people whose lives have been so wrecked by the effects of their parents' alcoholism. I start to see why I have been so angry and depressed all these years. And that brings me a little peace. A little peace is a start.

At my first meeting of this support group for families of alcoholics, I am stunned. Everyone is talking about *my life*. The confusion, anger, and self-loathing. The blaming, shaming, and guilt. I am so affected by all of this that I get physically ill and lose my voice for almost two months. This silence is a blessing; I need to learn how to write about my feelings. I need to be still and quiet. I need to listen. Thank God I don't need a voice to cry.

I am out of the basement. Out from under the table. On the way to living and feeling alive, maybe for the very first time.

THE TURNAROUND:

Being in Action as a Sane and Loving Parent

It's true: sanity brings sanity. I am slowing down and stepping off the ladder of success after decades of ninety-miles-an-hour, full-blast work addiction, and I have never felt greater joy or sanity. Sometimes I do feel a little queasy, as if my stomach has yet to match my slower pace.

I am a forty-year-old divorced mother of two—a recovering workaholic and alcoholic with an inherited predisposition toward creating toxic intensity and pumping out too much adrenaline. So I stay away from alcohol one day at a time and drink my fizzy water to avoid putting my children and myself through that particular hell that comes from being addicted to alcohol. I do my best to stay sane and to act sanely—to slow down, take deep breaths, and focus on what's really important. I work hard to stay in reality about money, watch for compulsive behaviors, and remember that most of what

I think I need I probably already have in the pantry, or the closet, or the new box of hand-me-downs for the children—if I just stop and think for a minute.

I am moving—moving my children and myself out of the high-priced house I bought as a workaholic mother and into a more affordable condominium—minus the fine china, nice jewelry, and backyard full of custom playscapes.

Moving away from thinking of life and parenting as something to be dealt with, I am embracing this opportunity and privilege with reverence, gratitude, humility, and, I hope, a healthy dose of humor as I learn to apply for scholarship money at the church day-care center.

Moving away from the intensity that comes from rushing to get everywhere, I choose to have some quiet time and just hang out or to call a friend for a "sanity check" on my spending plan for the week's groceries.

Cutting my working hours to six a day so I can spend more time with my children and manage my home more efficiently and effectively—though I'll probably still find soured towels in the washing machine every now and then.

Creating what truly brings me joy—a program to teach myself and other recovering parents the importance of self-care, asking for help, establishing boundaries, practicing money management—so you and I don't teach acceptance of toxic intensity, addiction, and insanity to our children.

Freeing myself from the urge to collect things—fine art, great china, unique jewelry. Instead, I create and collect great memories with my children—listening to my three-year-old name the worms she has just dug up and watching my six-year-old laugh himself silly over our Cheerios-eating pollywogs.

Stopping compulsive spending—to find fulfillment in creating order and stability and in asking, "What does sanity look like?" as I steadily head toward being debt-free.

Staying open to creating a loving relationship with a man who is mature, stable, wise, and funny—as opposed to thinking I need a driven Checkbook Charlie to provide me with a "secure future." Money doesn't equal security. Life is fragile, period. We have a much better opportunity to know security by building faith, love, and trust first. Money will follow, if it's meant to be.

I pray that I am making all these changes sanely and humbly and without the expectation that I can make this turnaround overnight. No doubt I will botch some important parenting challenges along the way. But I will do my best because I love my children and because in a spirit-filled moment I read and took totally to heart a quote from Jackie Kennedy, a quote that truly started my turnaround:

 If you botch raising your children, nothing else you do really matters.

In a holy moment of clarity, I taped that quote to my bathroom mirror and realized God had given me an opportunity to make things better. From that moment on, I knew that to raise my children, I must first respect and raise myself—every day.

So as I throttle down, drop back to punt, drop out, downsize and rightsize—financially, materially, spiritually, and emotionally—maybe sharing what's important to me will help you think about what's important to you.

Maybe, like me, you'll find it's important to look for ways to be more loving and respectful toward yourself by scheduling an extra fifteen minutes to get somewhere. Or you'll find ways to treasure your children more by remembering what it felt like to look into those little eyes for the first time. Perhaps if you're a mom who lives from drive-through to drive-through, you can find ways to take a deep breath and accept drive-through as the best you can do. Maybe that acceptance alone will bring joy and sanity into your life. After all, all your children really want is you—whether they're eating fries, PB and Js, or homemade whole-wheat pasta with garden-fresh tomato sauce.

All this said, my hope for you and me is sanity, serenity, love, and courage. And that today we will slow down. Breathe deeply. Be still and quiet. Grow in our own lives and gifts—and stay connected to them. When we take the time to do this, we are truly becoming TurnAround Moms.

Sane Ways to Live a Life of
Extreme Self-Care

❦

1. **URGENT—FIRST THINGS FIRST:** *If you are in an abusive relationship, get help immediately.* Call the **24-hour National Domestic Violence Hotline at 1-800-799-SAFE (7233) (TDD 1-800-787-3224)**. If you are afraid you could abuse your children, or if someone else in your family is harming your children, or if you are a child and you are being abused, call the **24-hour Childhelp National Child Abuse Hotline at 1-800-422-4453 (TDD 1-800-222-4453)**. Please don't waste a minute on this. If you need help, pick up the phone and call right now. (Please see the Resources section of this book for additional information.)

2. *If you are pregnant and drinking or using drugs, stop immediately and contact your doctor or health clinic.* Alcohol use during pregnancy is the leading known preventable cause of mental retardation and birth

defects. Your child will never "outgrow" this disability. No amount of alcohol use during pregnancy has been proven safe. Any woman who suspects she is pregnant, or is trying to get pregnant, should not drink. Period. This applies to all types of alcoholic beverages, including beer and wine. For more information, talk to your doctor. (Source: National Organization on Fetal Alcohol Syndrome. Please see the Resources section of this book for additional information.)

3. *If you think you or a family member has a problem with alcohol, drugs, or some other illegal, dangerous, or self-destructive behavior, ask for help right now.* About half the families in the United States are affected by alcoholism or drug abuse. Children who grow up in alcoholic families are four times more likely to become alcoholics. For help, start with the toll-free Alcoholics Anonymous number in your phone book, or visit the A.A. website at www.aa.org to find the A.A. and/or Al-Anon groups nearest you (Al-Anon is for families and friends of alcoholics). Members of A.A. are not there to judge you. They are there to stay sober themselves,

and one way they do that is by helping others get sober. A.A. and Al-Anon are home to some of the kindest, dearest, most generous, and successful people in the world. Give them, and yourself, a chance.

4. **Remember H.A.L.T.** If you are **H**ungry, **A**ngry, **L**onely, or **T**ired, take care of yourself right this minute, even before you read the next tip in this book. Ignoring any member of this unholy quartet can trigger behaviors you don't want or need. Taking care of yourself is crucial to your children as well. Remember, the airline flight attendant says, "In case of an emergency, mothers are required to put on their oxygen masks first, before giving masks to their children," because if you don't first save yourself, you can't save your children.

5. **Keep the focus on you and your children.** Make caring for yourself and your children your number one priority. You all need a healthy environment, good food, sane and loving friends and role models, spiritual guidance, honest work, and respect for your children's schoolwork.

6. ***Underpromise.*** Don't offer to do more than you can do. When you overpromise your time, energy, money, skills, or talents, you put yourself—and your family—at the disadvantage of owing someone something. This debt stacks up and can cost you—financially, emotionally, physically, and spiritually. Keep this negativism away from you and your family. Here's an example of under-promising: If you think you can be somewhere at 9:00 AM, just for the sake of taking care of yourself, say you'll be there at 9:30 AM. Then when you're early, you'll have time to focus, catch your breath, and give your full attention to the task at hand. Further, when asked to do something, it's best not to say yes in the moment. Instead say, "I'll have to get back to you," or "I need to check my calendar." This gives you time to see whether or not you can really take on something else—comfortably—before you commit.

7. ***Do something physically enjoyable for yourself every day: a bubble bath, a quick walk, dancing, or exercising to music you love.*** Give yourself a pep talk in the mirror with repeated affirmations such as "I am a beautiful

person" or "I am a sane and loving mother (or father)." Or simply dress nicely and put on hand lotion. Do something that helps you know you're taking care of yourself, especially when you're stressed. A fast-paced, ten-minute walk is a great stress breaker. As you walk, feel the power of your motion. A brisk walk can take you away from negativity and toward something positive because exercise helps your body release its own natural antidepressants. Exercise also helps regulate blood sugar, decreasing sugar-induced mood swings as well as cravings for sweets and starches.

8. *If self-pity starts creeping in, stop and create a gratitude list.* Write down ten things for which you're grateful. Start with the basics—clean water, food, shelter, people who care.

9. *Vote with your feet!* If something doesn't feel right, you don't have to explain—just walk away. Say no, and use the body language and actions that go with it. No is powerful and will keep you from overcommitting the precious time, energy, and money you need for yourself

and your children. When your children hear you say no, it teaches them to say no—to the wrong people, situations, drugs, and alcohol.

10. ***Take responsibility.*** When you can look at a problem and own up to your part in creating it, you're on your way to finding a solution. Drop the defensiveness. When you work toward a solution instead of staying stuck in a problem, your anger and resentment will dissolve, giving you a lot more energy to take care of yourself and your family.

11. ***If you're a perfectionist, give it up right now.*** Always trying to do everything exactly right is too much pressure on you and your children. Perfectionism is an enemy of sanity, causing some people to freeze up and do nothing! Practice saying, "Good enough," and "Good! Enough."

12. ***Important note to abuse survivors:*** If your children are young or if you are around young children, be aware that you may remember more intensely events that

happened to you when you were their age. In other words, children may trigger memories of your own childhood, especially as your children reach the age of your first conscious memory.

When my daughter turned five years old, I was suddenly aware of how vulnerable and innocent I was as a five-year-old when my father was abusive and violent. As an adult, I was angry about not having been protected.

2

Build a Strong
Support Structure

We can't do all of this—rear children, earn a living, learn how to be a sane and loving parent—alone. A strong support network is one of your greatest assets. It is okay to ask for help and for your children to see you do this. Asking for help is a sign of maturity. If you want your children to tell you when they need help, let them see you ask for help and advice in all types of situations—from moving furniture to working out money problems, from asking for directions to figuring out which home or apartment is best for you

to live in. It's good to have friends you can cry with,
cook with, travel with, and spend time with when you
need to be around strong, sane adults. Different friends
help with different problems; don't rely on one person
for everything. If you're early in recovery, people
understand that you'll probably need a lot of help
and won't be able to give back for quite a while.

THE PAIN STARTS HERE:

leaving Sleepy at Grandma's

My grandmother is always singing "There is a Balm in Gilead," "Amazing Grace," "Just a Closer Walk with Thee," and "What a Friend We Have in Jesus."

She stands there at her kitchen sink, peeling pears for preserves, and sings or hums those songs the whole time. It doesn't bother me the way it does when my little brother sings the same song over and over again. She just moves from one note to the next, one chore to the next, the music in her head carrying her along. And I love her so much.

We stay with her lots of weekends. I worry about Mother when we are at Grandma's. What is Daddy doing to her? Will she be okay when we get home, or will she have more bruises?

I am glad that at Grandma's there is almost always something to do outdoors to help take my mind off of things. My brother and I try to outsmart and catch those wild kittens that live in the garage. We pump icy water from the hand pump by the well house, or lie in the soft grass under the pecan trees that are part of Grandpa's orchard. We can also try to talk Grandma into letting us help pick strawberries or cut zinnias, or see if we can get Grandpa to let us ride in the back of his pickup truck on a trip down the bumpy dirt road to his fishing lakes (Brown's Lakes. Fish all day. $1.00).

Grandpa has false teeth that bother him. He also has a nub for one finger. "A mule bit it off," he tells us every time we visit.

I love to go to my grandma's almost anytime. Christmas Eve is most special, though. Grandma bakes ham, turkey, cornbread dressing, and those orange-peel cups filled with sweet potatoes and topped with crusty brown marshmallows. She hand grates every bit of coconut for her ambrosia, Japanese fruitcakes, and seven-layer cakes.

It's an incredible feast. The grown-ups eat in the dining room. My cousins and I eat in the kitchen. We're really too excited to eat, anyway. My cousin Rachel bosses us kids since she's oldest. We open presents and do our Christmas show of us children singing our holiday favorites: "Away in a Manger," "Silent Night," and "I Saw Mommy Kissing Santa Claus." The show is almost over when my little brother walks out with the picture of Daddy when he was in the navy. The picture has cotton on it in all the right places to make Daddy look like Santa Claus. My brother sings "Anchors Away." He's the only boy. Everybody loves his song.

All during the visit to Grandma's, Daddy slips out for quick slugs of his "Co-Cola"—half Coke, half Early Times bourbon—that he keeps in a Coke bottle in the car.

About midway through the present opening, my brother, cousins, and I start getting antsy, wanting to get out of our party clothes and hurry home to put out cookies for Santa.

Daddy's bourbon is making him a little too funny and a little too grumpy.

We are all glad when the final presents are handed out—Grandpa's little envelopes of money for the grown-ups. That means we're almost ready to go home, and Santa will be coming in just a few hours!

I believe I am remembering the Christmas when I was five. I have taken my most precious possession along with me to Grandma's: the stuffed bear I got last Christmas. He goes with me everywhere. I cannot sleep without him. His name is Sleepy. And he is the saddest bear in the history of the universe. Why Santa chose him, I'll never know. He has plastic ears and a plastic face frozen in a pitiful frown, with eyes that won't ever open and always look like they're bursting with tears. But I love him. And that night he is lost at Grandma's.

My brother and I fall asleep in the car on the way home, a trunkful of presents behind us, our parents snapping at each other in front of us. When we get home—about a twenty-minute ride—I wake up just enough to realize that I don't have Sleepy. And of course I pitch a fit. An irritable, snot-slinging "I can't go to sleep without him" fit.

I am wailing, "You have to go get him! What if he's not there?" And that takes my daddy and his Early Times all the way to rage.

Mother understands my hurt and calls Grandma to make sure Sleepy is there. He is. And then Mother sets out to drive across town to get Sleepy for me because I just can't go to sleep without him.

Daddy gets angrier. I am crying on my bed. He stands there with his belt in his hand and yells at me about how it will be my fault if Mother gets killed in a car wreck on the way to get my stupid bear. He tells me she could die in the dark out there on Christmas Eve. He says I am self-ish, and then he takes that big belt and whelps me good across the back of my thighs, all the while yelling at me, "Stop that crying, or I'll give you something to cry about!"

By the time Mother gets back with the bear I am sick. I've had Daddy's awful breath in my face yelling at me for a long time, and I am ready to throw up. I throw up a lot.

They fight. He goes at her with the belt and slaps her and pulls her hair. I cry. And I don't remember how it all ends that night, but there is Christmas the next morning. Somehow Santa got in and out without Daddy killing him. And in all the excitement of presents and new toys, nobody says anything at all about our night before Christmas.[1]

History Almost Repeats Itself: How Chicken Pox Cured a Nasty Case of Pride

It seemed my little son's skin acted out everybody's frustration; he got chicken pox a few days after I demanded that Bill leave. Then my daughter started breaking out with the pox just as her brother started clearing up. I had almost a month of spreading Calamine lotion on blistered skin, watching *Willy Wonka and the Chocolate Factory* 24/7, and singing the "oompa-loompa" song to a whimpering child.

Being a single mom with sick children is just damn hard, especially when you are single-handedly trying to earn a living, care for two pock-covered beings, and don't think you can change another diaper without turning green.

At the age of thirty-eight I was alone, afraid, and a nervous wreck. Adding to the stress, I was having a hard time accomplishing any work at all, and my intensely critical mother was quick to tell me that I was insane. She said I had destroyed the lives of her grandchildren by divorcing their father. The blisters on their skin seemed to be proof of what she was saying, though for the last couple of years she'd joined right in on commiserating with me about Bill's not helping out more financially. She seemed to forget all about that once he was gone.

It was in the midst of the confusion, fear, and resentment when I had the realization that I needed to get help to stop my self-destructive behaviors. I realized that with nobody around to stop me, I might start drinking, be unable to stop, and take my children down with me.

I was not a "big" drinker then, usually just those two beers while I cooked dinner. But often that was enough to rev up my anger and make me want to get on the phone and gripe instead of looking after my children or doing housework. The thought of a couple of beers turning into a nightly six-pack terrified me. I dreamed about the bruises, bald spots, and other ungodly things I'd seen and experienced at the hand of my alcoholic father by the time I was my son's age of five years. The stress of single parenting, running my own business, and juggling escalating credit card bills and a fat mortgage made the beer numb-out more attractive and more dangerous.

My children were devastated, angry, and confused by the divorce. At one point I wondered if I had set up my son to be as rageful as my father—or if this was yet another way to keep myself in the familiar, intense state of agitation—justification for a slip and deeper fall into my addictive behaviors.

Seeing my children in such pain was excruciating. It was a new bottom, and it was as far down as I wanted to go.

Just two years earlier, in my workaholic, spendaholic heyday, I was spending $1,500 a month for child care. Now, after this first month without Bill's help with the children, I was struggling hard to concentrate well enough to make $1,500 a month, much less pay it to sitters.

It was so tempting to knock the kids out with Benadryl, then knock myself out with a few drinks. It would be so easy, if I still had money, to plug in a babysitter and a bunch of videos for the children, and then go on a wild spending spree to outfit myself with new clothes, makeup, and assorted accessories.

It was a blessing that I couldn't buy my way out of this bleary-eyed fatigue with babysitters. It was a blessing that I realized I couldn't drink too much, or I'd run the risk of not being as alert as possible during those predawn oatmeal baths that calmed my children's raging skin. Seeing my children so vulnerable in their oatmeal baths scared me beyond belief. What if I got drunk and let them drown? That thought almost scared me to death. It almost scared me enough to stop drinking completely.

At times my imagination painted the picture of me going back home to my own mother, delivering my pock-covered children to stew in decades of unresolved conflict, and thereby creating another generation of toxic intensity and abuse. Dangerously depressed and overwhelmed, I could have let Mother take over our lives as I faded out of the way, convinced that I was incapable of caring for my children. Mired in self-pity and resentments, abusing alcohol and relationships, I would have added to her burden and burned her out, further alienating my stepfather. I imagined all of us sniping at one another, with me totally unable to take care of things.

Maybe it wouldn't have been that bad. I have no way of knowing. But I do know that at that time, Mother and I were so toxic for each other—quick to blame, shame, criticize, and fight—that my children did not need to be near the two of us together. I needed the eight-month break I took from talking to her to get my strength back, set boundaries, and be able to tell her to stop putting me down when we talked.

The reality? With just a few hours of paying project work on the books and the kids nearly clear of the pox, I had to get my life in order and generate some income. That's a tall order with a child under each wing. Especially when one is an angry five-year-old boy who's missing his dad and acting out his loss in fits of anger and rage.

I needed help with the children. Too tired to be proud, I was finally willing to ask for it, though I wasn't sure where to start. So I called a former client at our state's Council on Child Abuse. She sent a great guide for divorced parents. And she helped me to be creative about child-care options. I never imagined that these people I'd helped raise money for in my professional life could be so helpful in my private life.

Looking back, the pox upon our household brought some blessings. I was forced to slow down and be still with the children at the time when we all needed each other most. I was so alone, I finally had to set aside my workaholic, I-can-handle-anything pride. I had to find some help in dealing with toxicity and the temptation to abuse alcohol.

Asking for help outside of my family probably saved all of us—the children, my mother, and me—from scars far deeper than those left by the world's worst siege of chicken pox.

THE TURNAROUND:

Calling in the Saints

S urround yourself with sane people who love you."
That was the advice given to me by one of my
favorite priests when I told her I was going to get a
divorce. She gave me great comfort when she said, "God
doesn't want you to stay in something broken."

I understand now that God just plain doesn't want me
to be broken. If I'm broken, everything around me looks
broken.

Maybe if, while I was still married, I'd gotten into a
program that helps alcoholics and their families, or if I'd
known more about parenting and money management,
I wouldn't have been such a control freak, and Bill would
have had more freedom to succeed at his profession.
Then maybe my children wouldn't always be missing
somebody, whether it's me when they're with their dad,
or their dad when they're with me.

But that's not how it is. The three of us—the children and
I—started out twelve years ago with me feeling very broken.

If I chose to stay in the past and dwell on my misgivings, the children and I would never get anywhere, though sometimes it was extremely tempting to sit and beat myself up. Thank God, all along the way we've had wonderful people in our lives loving us and treating us as though we are worthy of love and acceptance. Thank God, some of them taught me that sitting and dwelling on the past is just another form of narcissism—an addiction to self-involvement that is best counteracted by awareness, acceptance, and getting into right action.

A friend recommended that I look for relief through a church-supported day-care center that could take both children from 8:30 AM until 6:00 PM. Fortunately, some of the children's friends were already there!

Mixed feelings of joy and sadness flooded over me on the children's first day at day care. I was so worn out; all I wanted to do was cry. We three had been through such a hard time, with them both sick almost the entire first month after I asked Bill to leave. But to have them both in a safe place with loving teachers and where they got a hot breakfast and a lunch with fresh vegetables—that I didn't have to cook—was more valuable to me than a winning lottery ticket. I had a lot of self-care to catch up on, and I couldn't rest, heal, recover, and generate an income with a five-year-old and an eighteen-month-old needing something every few minutes. To be any good to them, I had to be good to me.

So I took some of the time while they were at day care and went to support-group meetings for families of alcoholics. I started seeing the effect my father's alcoholism and mother's codependence to my father and his addiction had on my life. I learned that I didn't have to let those effects continue, that I could recognize and give up my own addictive and destructive behaviors. With God's help I could heal, grow, and be happy.

Structure. Time. Support. Saints. These blessings came from the day-care center and in the form of countless friends, coaches, and teachers. They all helped to make single parenting and my ongoing recovery from addictions and abuse possible. They helped to train, wear out, and inspire the best in my energetic children. They are saints who helped me learn to have some fun in my life, something my children never thought would happen.

Adult children of alcoholics are notorious for finding it hard just to have fun.

With all these support people in my life, I am constantly aware of how God works through his saints on earth. "I asked God for help, and he sent me other people," certainly rings true for me.

The lesson is this: If I'm willing to ask for the help, it's there. If I'm willing to take the leap of faith to admit I don't have all the answers, most of the answers come. They may not always be the answers I want, but this much I know about the biggest help there is: all in good time means all in God's time. If the help isn't there immediately, I must need more patience. If the help isn't quite enough, I must need to be more resourceful and responsible. If help shows up in some totally unexpected way, as it often does, I get to marvel at God's creativity and the way God always loves and provides, especially when I think I'm too broken to be loved.

Sane Ways to Build a
Support Structure

1. *Surround yourself and your family with families whom you admire, respect, and value.* Seek these families out at your church, synagogue, community center, school, or the local YMCA. Connect with these friends often. Discuss and create plans for how you can support one another with car pools, babysitting, house-sitting, errands, and such.

2. *If you're a new mom and you're home with a baby or a couple of little ones, avoid isolation.* Find a mothers' support group or a parent-child exercise class. Isolating is dangerous to your mental, physical, and spiritual health.

3. *If you feel uncomfortable or sick around someone, chances are he or she is a toxic person for you.* Avoid this person and others who evoke such discomfort.

4. ***Pick up the phone.*** It's one of your best tools to fight that feeling of being alone. Ask your friends and members of your support groups to be available for check-in calls, and to call you when they need to check in. Make check-in calls when you doubt yourself and need clarity, when you're losing your temper, or when you just need to say out loud what it is you want to do today. Call now if you need to.

5. ***If you have felt "down" for several weeks and can't seem to come out of feeling overwhelmed, seek professional help from a counselor, minister, priest, or rabbi.*** If you have health insurance, ask your insurance company to recommend a professional counselor. Whether you secure a counselor or not, check into the twelve-step programs in your area: Al-Anon for families of alcoholics; Alcoholics Anonymous; and other programs for overeaters, money mismanagers, and codependents. Ask for help; you do not have to suffer alone!

6. ***Avoid emergencies.*** Really. Build in a Plan B in every area you may need it: child care, housing, finances,

transportation. Keep this list of backups with you. Know who to call if your car fails, so you can get your children to school and yourself to work.

7. *At work, it's best and most professional to keep your troubles to yourself.* You're there to work, not give others information that could end up being used against you by an office gossip.

8. *Have at least one friend who can babysit for you and one professional child-care service you can call if you have a child who can't go to school or day care because of illness.* Yes, it's expensive. But single moms looking to build a record of stability on the job may find it less costly in the long run to pay for a trusted sitter than to miss a day at work. If you're secure in your job and can stay home, do so. Your love is one of the best medicines for your child.

9. *Avoid gossips and gossiping.* Gossiping creates anxiety and fear. Often people gossip to make other people look bad and make themselves look better, or just to keep a

conversation going. People who give up gossiping don't have to worry about what they said about somebody, or that things they said will come back to them and get them in trouble.

10. *Keep yourself and your children current or ahead on physicals, vaccinations, vision and hearing tests—as many types of health care as possible—so you can help identify and prevent health problems.* Prevention and early detection save time, pain, and money. Get to know your doctors and nurses. Take your children to free screenings for vision, hearing, blood pressure, diabetes—anything being offered by a reputable health organization.

3

Create a Sane
and Loving Family Life

The more we practice self-discipline and self-control, the greater the likelihood that our children will be able to practice self-discipline and self-control. The more we create sanity, peace, and calm, the greater the likelihood that they will create sanity, peace, and calm for themselves. If we have family time that encourages respect and communication, our children will be respectful and know how to communicate well. We cannot say we love someone and criticize them in the same breath. Chaos and criticism create opportunities for more chaos and criticism. If we want someone to stop yelling, sometimes we have to start whispering, or say nothing at all, because the fastest way to end an argument is to stop arguing. A few minutes of quiet time together before bed means everyone will get a better night's sleep. Reading and saying nightly prayers together is a routine that's good for children and parents; it creates an appreciation of sanity, serenity, and togetherness.

THE PAIN STARTS HERE:

it was Shake 'N Bake and I yelped

The word "vacation" has two sides to it. There is the getting excited about going somewhere, with the packing and the thoughts of swimming and playing in the ocean and seeing our older cousins. Then there's the other side. The actual going on vacation. And for me, at age eight, it's kind of scary.

Our family vacation is usually a blitz to Panama City, Florida, for white beaches, cheap seafood, and a swimming pool at the Holiday Inn. There are crabs to try to catch, which is our favorite pastime. And there's a strip of cheesy amusements called the Miracle Mile. Going to the Miracle Mile is supposed to be our reward for good behavior, but we never make it there, even if we are good.

The drive to Florida is usually not too awful. Knowing that I get carsick just riding around the block, Mother doses my brother and me with Dramamine, and we don't wake up until we are a couple of hours away. Then the other side of the vacation starts. I need to go to the bathroom, and Daddy, who's already had a "Co-Cola" or two, meaning a Coke with a load of bourbon in it, is hell-bent to stay on the road. Mother begs me to hold it. And then when I just can't anymore, Daddy stops by the side of the road, and I jump out to "tinkle," trying to keep from being seen by folks driving up the road, and trying to keep the spray and dust from splashing up on my ankles and shorts.

Once we're there, Mother meets up with her sister, Aunt Faun, and starts telling her the latest gossip and stories about Daddy's drinking. Daddy goes deep-sea fishing—one of the best ways ever to stay away from Mother and us all day and get rip-roaring, upchucking drunk. Uncle James and my cousin Dottie take us to the pool, so we can start on our blister-and-bleed sunburns.

At night, we go to Captain Anderson's, Daddy's favorite place to eat and drink himself senseless—and the scene of much acting-out by my brother and me. For starters, I've perfected a routine in which I act retarded. I drag a leg, curl an arm, slur words, and dribble spit down my chin before pawing a stranger and saying, "Do you have a quarter?" My brother does this, too. We think it is hilarious. And my parents let us do it. And they laugh. I feel sad about that now. I feel sad and ashamed that we made fun of people.

At bedtime, Daddy, overweight, drunk, sweaty, and puffing on a big nasty stogie, cranks the room air conditioner down to meat-locker cool. And since my meat has cooked all day in the Florida sun, the contrast is painful. Racked with chills, I shake, shiver, cry, and ask for more blankets. Mother tries to put lotion on me, cover me up, and shut me up. Daddy gets annoyed about us "whining little pissants" and then knocks Mother around for a while. Finally, things settle down, and we get a little sleep.

The next day, we wake up feeling good enough to go outside and explore. And refry ourselves. So there's another day of baking, bitching, boozing (Daddy), and then bingeing on Captain Anderson's famous red snapper, the king of fish, and as many onion rings as we can choke down.

After three days of this, I am usually sick with bronchitis. Some of the sun blisters bleed. And Daddy is in an almost constant state of agitation, drinking, fighting. Then he buys us stuff to try to make up for being so mean.

It is an intense cycle. It is what my brother and I know. We never think that it might not be normal. When you're a little kid, you think everybody does the same things you do.

Finally, it's time to go home. Huddled in the backseat of our air-conditioned car, I try to stay warm. It is ironic as hell. It *is* hell. Outside it is 100 degrees. In our car, it is so cold you can almost see your breath. And then, to top it all off, Daddy lights another fat cigar, takes off his shirt, locks down the pedal, and does his best to get us home quickly, so he can hook up with his drinking buddies and rid himself of his weak children and bitchy wife.

By the time we get home I have a high fever. After Mother takes me to get a fannyful of penicillin, I'm in bed for four or five days to recover from all this family fun.

This vacation insanity happens again and again. On the way to Canada, Daddy turns the car around in a blaze of rage—within spitting distance of our Niagara Falls destination—and drives straight back to Georgia. This time I have pneumonia. Another time, in Mexico, after Daddy discovers a drink called the Zombie, we all turn into the walking dead.

I will never forget the incredible sadness I feel for my brother, who is eight or nine, during the Zombie trip. We are eating supper at the hotel's alfresco restaurant and saloon. Drunk and bragging about his business successes, Daddy buys drinks for people up and down the bar—gives fifty dollars to a total stranger. And then, when he needs to go to the bathroom, he has to ask my little brother for help. And here is this child—red hair, freckles, cute little suit—helping this huge, tottering man look for the toilet.

Careening off the wall, Daddy keeps talking about needing to "take a leak." Finally, he can't move anymore until he pees. So he unzips his pants in front of the people he's been bragging to, pulls out his giant penis, and urinates all over the wall as my brother tries to hold him up. I don't know what Mother is doing. I am looking at my brother, who is so embarrassed that his face is on fire, and his eyes are filled with tears. There is the urge to cry. And the urge to laugh. But mostly there is the urge to get the hell out of there. The bad news is Daddy is drunk again. The good news is that he's too drunk to beat up Mother.

At daylight, we load Daddy into the back of the station wagon. Mother climbs behind the wheel. And I don't remember stopping for anything but gas and the bathroom until we make it home to Georgia.

This might be the last time we try to go anywhere as a family. And I am fine with that. It is more family fun than I need or want. I appreciate the valuable lessons I learned. Even when you're not happy, you can learn a lot: how not to have a family vacation and how alcoholism is a disease that kills even the best of intentions—and what should be the happiest of times.

History Almost Repeats Itself: The Sober Thanksgiving

My boyfriend, Bryan, is driving like a maniac, zigging and zagging between cars. He's mad as hell at himself for running late. Tiny beads of sweat dot his tan brow. Hands drum the steering wheel. The smoked hams he's bringing as his contribution to the feast smell divine, though he's worried that they are not enough. Meanwhile, my children are in the backseat, laughing, giggling, doing children things. And this infuriates him.

We are on the way to Thanksgiving dinner at the home of Bryan's aunt. She is his ideal woman: tall, beautifully groomed, filthy rich, and really, really sweet. She and her husband live in a magnificent house in a ritzy development. The basketball hoop in the driveway catches Kenny's eye the minute we drive up.

The children are great at lunch—well-mannered, good appetites, and friendly in this houseful of people they've met either just once or never before. Kenny and Sophie love the aunt's little dogs and the crate the dogs live in. They entertain themselves most of the day by playing with the dogs and playing house in the crate.

After lunch we're to meet my ex-husband so the children can spend the rest of the holiday with him and his fiancée. It's not too far to travel, but Bryan is in his usual hurry. He wants to get my children dropped off quickly, so he can spend more time with his family. He joins in Kenny's basketball practice for a minute or two, then stops it suddenly with orders to load up and go.

On the road, the children are doing that laughing thing again. Bryan wants peace and quiet. He's concentrating on how to get to where we're meeting Bill and Kate.

We don't find them at the first place we thought they'd be. As it turns out, there's another gas station of this description about fifteen miles farther up the road. I call Bill on the cell phone. Bryan is irritated because we've driven more than halfway to meet Bill. The farther we go, the more irritated he gets. Finally, he can't stand it any longer and turns around and yells at the children to shut up. They have been rambunctious, but not obnoxious. They're children. They're excited about seeing their dad.

Bryan and I were better together during the summer when the children were with their dad in Florida. But now that they're back, the rivalry between Kenny and Bryan is intense. Bryan's lack of patience and driving intensity—and intensity while driving—are too much for me. And I am grateful to be noticing all of this.

We finally meet Bill and Kate at the right gas station. Bryan can barely look at Bill; he is so angry about being "ripped off" on meeting "halfway." We get back in his car, and he unloads his anger on me. About how disrespectful my children are. How my ex-husband takes advantage of us. How I am "not in control" of my children. He keeps saying over and over that I am not paying attention to him. I repeat what he says, so he knows I've heard him. He finally takes my jacket by the scruff of the neck and shakes me to bring home the point that I need to be shaken awake so I'll see how I let the kids and Bill "take me for a fool."

If we weren't on a country road in the dark on a chilly November night, I'd get out of the car. But I'm not stupid. The object of the exercise now is to get home. And dump this guy as fast as I can.

Back at his aunt's home, some of the family is getting ready to leave. More irritation on Bryan's part because he's missed time with them. His uncle and cousin are spending the night. So the late-night folks gather in the living room and pour up some brandy. I am not drinking, thank God. I've been in a support group for families of alcoholics for four years. And for the last year, I've also attended a program for alcoholics who want to stop drinking. It's been six months since I've had a beer, and I am grateful to be wide awake, alert, attentive, and sober. I want to go home.

Finally, it is time to go. On the long trip back Bryan starts ranting about the children again.

"Those kids just take you for an idiot. They really do. You let them push you around."

"My daddy would have taken off his belt to me if I'd acted like your kids."

"They are totally out of control. How can you let those two disrespect you like that?"

"If I didn't love you so much it wouldn't matter. But I love you and hate to see those children treat you that way."

He is talking about a five-year-old and an eight-year-old who were giggling in the backseat—children who received numerous compliments for their manners during lunch. Children who were excited to see their dad for the first time in several weeks. Children who are loving and kind and who said, "Thank you" for their lunch without being asked. Children who were in a house full of breakables and strangers and didn't break a thing or offend anyone—except Bryan.

Bryan is also, I recall, grieving the death of his father (eight months earlier) with the help of six beers and a snifter of brandy. I admit, I counted his beers. I admit, too, that I probably should have forced the issue to appoint myself the designated driver on the way home.

At his place, I go in. I am so overcome with fear and

the weight of the denial I've been carrying around that I can barely speak. By the end of the holiday weekend, all of the things he's lent me are back at his house, and he's returned my things to me. He's angry and miserable about the breakup. Tries to patch it all up. And I am firm. Strong. Praying he'll just go away and leave us alone.

When the children get home on Sunday, I tell them they won't be seeing Bryan anymore, and they are thrilled. And I am grateful. Grateful that I didn't even have the first taste of beer that night at his aunt's, because even one beer would have been enough to keep the denial and the toxic intensity going. One would have been enough to gloss over my fear of his rage. One could have been enough to make me kiss and make up. The bottom line? Sobriety saves lives—and makes life worth saving.

This is a real Thanksgiving.

THE TURNAROUND:

Arizona Treasures

The children and I are on the vacation of a lifetime. Truly, I have always wanted a real vacation. So my two beautiful children and I are going to Arizona to have some fun. With God's help, I have sold the house, moved, gotten the children back from their dad's where they've been for the past three weeks, packed for the trip, and gotten us out here—in ten day's time.

We are staying at Kenny's godmother's house. A friend of fifteen years, she adores Kenny and has opened her home to us for a month. We've not been here five minutes when she shows me a little clipping from the local paper: "Elden Pueblo Dig Open to Public."

Kenny says he wants to be an archaeologist. He is enamored of Indiana Jones (*Raiders of the Lost Ark*) and all things old. This public dig—an infrequent occurrence here—has divine timing. It is also an opportunity to support my child in pursuing his dream and to do something that is deeply important to me: heal some of the sadness I've felt about how horrible vacations were for me as a child by creating pleasant memories of vacation time with my own children.

On the first day of the dig, I am still tired from all the effort of getting to Arizona. We go to the site late in the afternoon and stay for an hour and a half, long enough to meet some of the people and let the children become truly interested in what is happening. They love the trowels, whisk brooms, dustpans, and buckets of dirt. Their eyes light up as a tall excavation volunteer stands and screens a pile of rock-filled earth.

The children are into this in a big way. Kenny becomes attached to one particular digger. His name is Walt, and it is fine with this patient man to have my seven-year-old tag along behind him for a while. Kenny loves Walt. Sophie hugs his leg. Walt invites us to come back, so our plans are set for the following Sunday.

As the next dig day draws near, Kenny makes plans to prepare lunch for Walt. He is going to take tuna sand-wiches, apples, and bottles of frozen water. He is wearing the T-shirt I bought for him at the dig last week. He is so excited about going back to the Elden Pueblo dig that he has not worn another shirt for five days.

We arrive at the dig, and Kenny, lunches in hand, takes off to find the room Walt and his colleagues are reconstructing. Walt seems glad enough to see Kenny. Sophie falls in line with her brother, and the two of them start asking questions. Foolishly, I think I can sit under a tree and write while they dig. Instead, I keep a constant check on the children, making sure they're getting enough water and not actually destroying anything with these beloved tools.

As the day ends, Kenny says a reluctant good-bye to

his friends. Walking down the trail to the car, he spots some ancient pottery on a rock. It's not right to be a pot-snatcher, a creepy person who steals relics. Kenny knows that, even though it would be cool to own a piece of three-hundred-year-old pottery, the right thing to do is to take it to Walt.

I keep silent. And without saying a word, this little boy, who has tried to find relics like these all day, picks up the treasures and turns around. He walks back up the long trail. I watch as he turns the antiquities over to Walt. I see Walt nod and give Kenny a hug. I pick up Sophie and tell her that her brother has just made us very proud.

Later during this trip, we go on missions to find blue crawfish in a remote swimming hole called Wet Beaver Creek. We spend a day driving through the desert to the Grand Canyon, and Kenny stays awake with me as we drive back late on a night so clear we see stars and planets I've never seen before. On this night Kenny asks, "Mom, will you please not play the Deepak Chopra tape again?" And he holds my hand for about a hundred miles, while his sister sleeps soundly.

We catch and release a horned toad not much bigger than my thumbnail. We do laundry and go grocery shopping and take care of his godmother's cats and dog and go to her church for an outdoor service where the children climb trees and Sophie gets scratched by a wild kitten.

We catch trout in the forest and watch an electrical storm in Sedona, where we walk into every bookstore in town searching for a children's book on survival in the wilderness—written by a real Indian. And we find it, too.

We attend a couple of support group meetings for families of alcoholics and are touched by the warm welcome we receive from people who go from strangers to friends in less than an hour.

We charge through three airports on the way home, Sophie sitting on the back of the rolling luggage cart and Kenny holding my hand, both of us loving how much Sophie delights in the ride.

This vacation is a redeeming experience for me. I love being able to help my children create wonderful memories of our adventures. It is the beginning of my biggest adventure yet: life as a sane and sober single mother.

Stressed at times. But blessed beyond belief to have the freedom of traveling with two healthy, inquisitive children. It is what I hope will be the first of many long vacations—away from phones, pressures, and things that sometimes manage to keep us apart no matter how hard we try to stay connected.

I have learned how to take the kind of family vacation I'd always dreamed of, and how to bring that kind of joy and sanity home to stay. There are no better keepsakes.

Sane Ways to Parent and Create a Loving Home Life

❧

1. *If you don't like something your children are doing, look at yourself to see if it's something **you** need to stop doing.* For instance, if I want my children to have a clean workspace, I need to have a clean workspace. Lead by example. Ask yourself as you go through a yellow light, eat an extra slice of cake, say something less than kind about a friend: "Would I want my children to do what I'm doing now?"

2. *Greet each day joyfully and optimistically.* Let your children see you do this.

3. *Instead of reacting, learn how to de-escalate and respond.* Reacting means you yell, strike, or speak out without thought. Reacting can create more to "clean up." Reacting keeps you in the problem. De-escalating means reducing the level of intensity in a situation by

speaking slowly and quietly. Responding means that you think before you speak, take a breath, and stop yourself from lashing out. You come from a saner place. De-escalating and responding work toward a solution. And remember: sometimes the best response is no response. You can end an argument quickly by calmly walking away. Wait to respond until you've had the chance to think through the situation and discharge the anger.

4. *Live in a consequence-based home.* Lay out the choices and the consequences in advance, and make them stick. Homework not done? No free time. Chores not done? No TV. Stick to your consequences and you'll realize another benefit: your children will start paying better attention to you, so you won't have to repeat yourself. Further, children with limits feel safer and more secure.

5. *Starting right now, do your best not to rush yourself or your children.* To "create" more time, plan ahead, get everyone up earlier, and leave earlier. Rushing is abusive.

6. ***Children spell love T-I-M-E.*** Spend time—all kinds of
time—with your children. Giving them time, attention, guidance, and consequences helps them to feel
worthy and important. Children who feel worthy and
important are better able to say no to risky situations
because they value themselves too much to be self-
destructive. The best time of the day together can be
the five to thirty minutes before bedtime, when you
and your children are quiet and peaceful as you read to
them, say prayers, or both. A few minutes of peaceful,
connected time just before bed goes a long way toward
helping everyone feel loved and secure.

7. ***Every now and then stop and really, really, really look
into the eyes of your children.*** Remember what it felt
like to do this the very first time, how in awe you were
of this tiny, helpless, totally dependent being. Em-
pathize. Try to imagine how you would feel if you were
as young and helpless as your children are now. Use
words and actions that show reverence and respect for
yourself *and* your children. It is harder to mistreat or
abuse those you honor.

8. ***Remember the things you most hated about how you were brought up.*** Guilt? Shame? Blame? Judgment? Write them down. Look at them for a while. Then earnestly ask God, or whatever you call your Higher Power, to help you give up those behaviors and not allow yourself to be affected by that kind of negativism. Once you've done this, either tear up the list and flush it down the toilet or burn it in a safe place. It may seem silly to destroy that sheet of paper in such a dramatic way, but there's energy in saying you're going to break negative traditions, asking for those behaviors to be removed, then turning the list into sewage or ashes.

9. ***Remember the maxim of Stephen Covey, author and founder of the Covey Leadership Center, "It's easier to change your attitude about your child than it is to change your child."*** It's amazing how much better life is when you look for the things your children do right instead of the things they do wrong. When you notice the good things your children do—going for thirty minutes without arguing, brushing their teeth without being asked, remembering to take out the garbage—

you build on the positive feelings in your family life. Get in the habit of praising your children, and mention the exact reason they are being praised. This makes the compliments more authentic and memorable to you and your children. At the same time, you must balance the need for limits and consequences, as all praise and no self-control can create spoiled, self-righteous children.

10. ***Adult children of alcoholics and/or people who grew up in other abusive situations sometimes have a hard time knowing how to discipline their children.*** We are afraid that if we discipline too hard, we could become abusive. Some of us err on the side of being so loving that we are weak when it comes to establishing rules and carrying through on consequences. One solution is to find other parents whose children are responsible, well-mannered, and doing well in school. I ask these parents in advance how they would handle situations requiring consequences, and then I call them when I'm stumped. I rotate the calls, so I don't lean on any one person too heavily. Reading books on parenting helps,

too, though the calls help me most to see whether or not I'm over- or underresponding.

11. ***Irritable?*** Irritability is a sign your needs are not getting met. When you learn how to make direct requests for what you need and want, and start getting more of your needs met, you'll be gentler with yourself and with your children. One way to simplify making direct requests is to standardize the ongoing "house rules and requests." If your children are old enough to read, write down and refer to these guidelines so children know what is and is not acceptable behavior. This keeps you from wasting energy by repeating yourself.

12. ***Hold a "family meeting" at the same time each week.*** Sunday evenings work well for my family. Lay out on a calendar what's coming up for each family member: practices, rehearsals, special school projects, field trips, and so on. This way you're more likely to know on Sunday that somebody needs Play-Doh for a model of the solar system due on Friday, instead of finding out Thursday night just as the stores close. This kind

of planning and communication helps prevent disasters and allows everyone the chance to be heard at least once a week. (Have a no-interrupt rule, so everyone gets to voice their concerns without being silenced by an older sibling.) You can use this time to discuss family schedules, menus, budgets, vacation plans, and special needs, as well as to take a look at what went well the week before, what caused problems, and how you can work together to find solutions. Children love the routine. Add to the ritual by serving a simple food that's a family favorite, and your family will associate pleasure with the meeting, making it all the more productive.

Of Special Importance to Abuse Survivors

Be prepared when your child hits the age of four or five, or whatever age it is that you first remember abuse. It is likely that you will see yourself in your child, and you will be stunned that anyone could hurt that innocent little person. When Sophie turned five, I plunged into a deep depression, thinking about how horrific it would be for her to have seen what I saw at her age and that when I was her age I did see those things. Fortunately, a close friend who had been abused as a child told me the same thing had happened to her when her daughter turned five. In fact, she wrecked her car. I was greatly comforted when this friend explained that it's not unusual for this feeling of déjà vu to happen.

We project our own experiences onto our children. We realize we could not bear for our precious children to be harmed as we were. We also feel such anger that the people we loved—our parents—were not protecting us and were, in fact, placing us in dangerous situations when we were at that same age. It is stunning. Shocking. Anger-evoking. Depression-evoking. If you are not careful, it can really hurt you. This is why it is important to seek help—counseling, Al-Anon if appropriate, a survivors' group, something—before your child hits that age. Being prepared for this experience is part of the reason why this re-parenting of yourself is so essential: You learn how to practice excellent self-care, it is healing for you, and it sets a great example for your children.

Further, if you are lucky enough to have grandchildren, the same thing is likely to happen when your same-sex grandchild becomes the same age you were when you had your first conscious memory of the abuse. Although I am not a grandmother yet, I know this because I've watched friends with grandchildren experience it.

This is crucially important to remember. It is almost as though there should be a warning label on your child(ren) and grandchildren when they are born: YOU WILL HAVE TO RELIVE PARTS OF YOUR CHILDHOOD AS YOU RAISE YOUR CHILD. When your child reaches the age(s) of your greatest abuse, disappointment, shame, rage, whatever, you are likely to reexperience those feelings. Be prepared, get help, and be gentle on yourself and your family.

4

Establish and Keep Strong Boundaries

The stronger we make our boundaries, the better we make our lives. The limits we place on others determine the way people treat us; people with strong boundaries don't allow others to abuse them. By watching us, our children learn to create and maintain strong boundaries for themselves. It's a two-way street, though—we have to honor the boundaries of others and let our children see us do that as well. When we consistently honor boundaries, children begin to understand the connection between self-respect and treating others respectfully.

When we respect ourselves, it is easier to respect others. I have trouble with being on time. My children are a lot more disciplined about time when I am disciplined about it and "walk the walk" instead of just saying, "We've got to do better about this." Honoring boundaries works in all areas of our lives. We can't expect our children to do something we're not willing to do ourselves.

THE PAIN STARTS HERE:

beauty hurts

No matter what clothes I have on or how I've done my hair or what I am doing, I am just not right. Mother wants my hair curly. It is straight. So we go to Lucie's Beauty Parlor, and I get those little permanent-wave curlers in my hair. Lucie puts that stinky, rotten-egg-smelling stuff all over my head, and my hair looks fried and frizzy, like the hair on a doll that's been in the swimming pool and left out in the sun. And I hate it.

The sponge rollers—those pink things with rods that always catch a few stray hairs and pull them when the clasp goes "snap"—go on my head almost every night. Mother comes in and rolls my hair, and I am miserable. The next morning some of the curlers have come out, and part of my hair is so short and curly it's above my ears while the rest of it hangs straight and stringy down the back of my neck. Mother says, "Your hair is stringy."

The worst case of Mother's trying to control my hair was one Christmas when Aunt Faun, Mother's sister, was visiting. Mother lit in to me about my not combing my stringy hair and how horrible it looked. I took my school scissors and cut a big chunk of it off up to my scalp and then cried and cried. I was so mad. Aunt Faun, bless her, came in my room and cut my hair into a kind of a pixie cut that would get me through Christmas until Mother could take me back to Lucie's.

Clothes weren't as bad as hair, but they were bad enough. I couldn't match them or fit them or be in them the right way no matter what. Everything was always getting tugged at and adjusted or pulled down or retied or wiped off with a wet washcloth that stayed on the front seat of the car and smelled like the bottom of the clothes hamper.

One Christmas I went beyond feeling embarrassed and annoyed to being totally ashamed. I guess I was about eight.

Santa Claus brought me a bra and panties set, blue

with little pink flowers on the straps. I noticed that some girls in fourth grade were getting bosoms, and I thought it was pretty neat to have that little bra—until Mother and Daddy made me put it on and *wanted to see me in it!* Mother fixed my hair and put lipstick on me. And they took my picture, all posed up with one foot pointing down and one finger in the air. I felt so stupid, ashamed, and embarrassed, I wanted to die. I don't know if anybody other than my little brother was around. I wanted to cry every time I looked at that picture.

As the years went by, the comments about my appearance never let up. I was always too skinny. Daddy laughed about my flat chest and said that with my big, bony shoulder blades I looked more like a girl from the back than from the front. Sometimes he'd get mad at me about my posture. He'd almost bend me over backward as he dug his thumbs into the ends of my shoulder blades, trying to stick them back in.

When my cousins, who were about my same age, got breasts and I didn't, it was even worse. I could almost feel him staring at my chest, wondering when "those little walnuts like Sue and Rachel have are gonna pop up on you."

He never got the chance to find out. Because he kept on drinking, beating up Mother, and saying ugly things to me, I told Mother she had to divorce him or I was leaving. She finally did when I was almost fifteen. I didn't get my period or any little bit of breasts until after he was long gone. I guess my body had its own biological boundaries.

My mother is a beautiful woman. She has a great figure. She takes a lot of time getting herself dressed for church. Looking good is important to her. My looking good is important to her, too. When she and Daddy were married, his shirts were always pressed, his pants had creases in the right places, and his socks usually matched. His looking good was important to her. Together they were masters at looking good on the outside, while inside our home continued to crumble.

History Almost Repeats Itself:
The Great Thanksgiving War That Wasn't

I hoped it was going to be a peaceful Thanksgiving. Mother and my stepfather, Harold, were coming for a late lunch at the restaurant in my condominium complex. The kids and I had gone where I go for support-group meetings for an early Thanksgiving celebration. We didn't eat much, knowing we'd better be hungry when Mother and Harold took us out.

She and Harold showed up a little early. We were all getting ready to go. Not that we were dressing up much. It was a casual dining place—a place where golfers and their families would grab a burger and a soda. But today they were having a nice Thanksgiving buffet, and I was glad to be skipping the drive to Mother's with the children. I think she was glad that my stepfather was buying lunch, so there wouldn't be all the cooking to do.

I had just run upstairs to help Sophie find something when it happened. I heard a little boy screaming and an old woman yelling. I bolted down the stairs to find my son in tears and my mother steaming.

"I'm not taking him to lunch in that shirt! He ought to know better than to wear a shirt like that out of his house. That looks awful! He doesn't have any pride about himself whatsoever, does he? Why, I'd be embarrassed to go somewhere with my grandmother looking like that. . . ."

It took me about five seconds to clear my head and put my "what was happening" and "what was said" test over the scene of a seven-year-old boy being shamed by a seventy-one-year-old woman. And I felt it come up inside me and come pouring out: the desire never to see my children hurt or shamed or blamed for anything, but especially not something as minor as an imperfect shirt.

No guilt. No shame. No blame. That's what the sign on my kitchen cabinet door says. And I mean it.

Mother wasn't backing down about the shirt. It was as though she wanted me to jump into the fray—on her side. I took a deep breath and told her that she could leave if she wanted to, but that this was my home. I remember, vividly, saying something I'd wanted to say to Mother for years, something along the lines of "In my home children do not get shamed. If you say one more word to this child about the clothes he has on or about his appearance, you can leave and we will forget Thanksgiving lunch."

Kenny joined in, tears streaming down his face, and yelled, "I hate you, Meemaw!"

That wasn't acceptable, either. I told him to have a seat. I took a deep breath and asked God for help. Then

I proposed that Mother and Harold take their car down the hill to the restaurant and that we would follow. But I added that if one more critical word—about anybody or anything—came out of either of their mouths, they could have lunch at the restaurant and we would go home for peanut butter and jelly sandwiches in peace.

The ride down the hill—in separate cars—helped a lot. We ate lunch on dull pins and needles, mindful of the boundaries in talking about appearances and manners. We finally began to enjoy one another right about the time we were eating dessert, when Harold started talking about the Great Depression and how hamburgers cost a nickel then and how poor everybody was.

Kenny was fascinated. Mother talked about how she had chopped cotton in Alabama and how hard it was to fill one of those long croker sacks with cotton bolls. How she, her brothers, and sister had to take such good care of their clothes and shoes because they might not get any more for another year or two. Different generations. Different values. Mother's "Take care of what you have and look your best so people won't know you're poor as dirt" versus my "It's just a thing. Don't worry about spilling something on it; it's what's inside the shirt that counts."

It was a Thanksgiving that could have turned into a cause for not speaking for a while, but instead, because of my newfound ability to take a deep breath, set boundaries, and start life over, and Mother's decision to stay in the conversation, the day turned into the best of what family time is all about: trying to understand our differences, looking beyond snap judgments, and somehow, between the first deviled egg and the last bite of pie, deciding we're pretty lucky to have one another after all.

THE TURNAROUND:

I Can't Lose—or Win—the Game All by Myself

I nearly let a work situation get the best of me one Friday. Violating my own rules to take extra care of myself when I'm worn out and feeling overly sensitive, I went to the office when it would have been smarter to take the all-too-rare mental health day and stay home alone. I failed to honor a self-care boundary to rest and recharge myself so I have the capacity to be creative and discerning.

Fear drove me on to work. Fear that there'd be something I'd need to explain or revise. Fear that not being there would "look bad." Fear that I hadn't had a "win" with this particularly exasperating project for almost six weeks.

At the office I learned that the project wasn't mine anymore. My boss was taking it over. More senior-level people were being brought in for a meeting that afternoon to handle all tasks relating to this client, and I wasn't asked to attend the meeting. Already tired and vulnerable, I let myself start interpreting their choices instead of just accepting that I'm in trouble; I botched it up; nobody values what I have to say about this. The day became a miserably twitchy mess of guilt and insecurity as I even took the horrible feeling to my son's ball game that night.

At the bottom of the sixth in a six-inning game, Kenny was called to the plate with the scoreboard flashing two outs and the sad score of six to four. He swung.

He missed. Strike one. The ball zoomed over home plate. He didn't swing. Strike two. On the next pitch, he swung so hard I was afraid his arm and shoulder might fly off with the bat. He missed. Strike three. He's out. Afterward the tears came.

"I lost the game for us, Mom."

"No, you didn't, son. There were eight other players on your team, and you were all playing in the same game."

"Doesn't matter. I was the last at bat. I lost it. I struck out."

"You struck out. You didn't lose the game."

More tears. A hug. And the realization that I had been thinking and acting out almost the same thing all day. I was no more the total cause of the problem with my former project than Kenny's strikeout was the only reason his team lost the game. He was just the last one at bat; I was just the one with the earliest—and most—exposure to the project. My boss and a team of designers and account people were working on the assignment, too. We had been together every step of the way. They knew the client was challenging, redefining this incredibly complex product at least every other day.

So that night, after Kenny's game and my shutout at work, he and I were irritable, anxious, and exhausted.

The next day, at the last game of the season, Kenny got two solid hits and fielded beautifully. He pitched the last inning—a strike, another strike, and an easy-out pop fly. He was thrilled. I was still "hungover" from my emotional, fear-filled Friday.

Over the weekend I talked with a couple of friends about the work situation. Cried. Reasoned things out. I told the story about the mirrorlike reactions Kenny had to his striking out and I had to being benched at work.

God doesn't fool around with me. If he wants me to stop doing something that hurts me, I'll soon see the destructive behavior in my children. In my world, it seems to be a law of the universe: what I don't face head-on in myself, my children will have to face.

Like most moms, I'll certainly do for my children what I'm not always willing to do for myself. I'll take care of myself, so Kenny and Sophie will learn how to take care of themselves. I'll set boundaries with myself and with others and ask for help with my runaway fear. I'm more willing than ever to practice this extreme self-care because I know that if I don't want my kids in the man-against-self boxing ring, I've got to be willing to stop my own pain.

The next Monday I countered my depression with the best cures I know: self-care in the form of eight hours of sleep the night before, prayer, exercise, a good breakfast, and considered action to strengthen my boundaries.

First, I went to see my boss and told her that I accepted my part in not asking for more help and for not starting to write sooner, even if I didn't have all the information I'd asked for. I told her that in the future I would raise my hand earlier if things didn't seem to flow. Then I made a request. I asked her point-blank to do what she could to prevent my becoming the scapegoat on this out-of-control project.

I asked her to stand up for me, to answer criticism with the truth that the writers need more support in leading and managing client expectations. I told her it was important to me that she not let me take the fall alone. She acknowledged that I had gotten some of the blame and promised to watch out for scapegoating. I knew she would honor my request.

Later, as I wrote about this situation in my journal to help me process it, put it in perspective, and not repeat it, my son was fast asleep. And I realized that I have more to be thankful for than any scoreboard or profit-and-loss sheet in the world can track: A healthy family. A healthier relationship with my mother. A great church community. Wonderful friends. God's gifts of reason, healing, and courage. Knowledge about how to create and maintain healthy boundaries.

Next time, God willing, I'll have the courage to recharge my discernment and creativity batteries way before I'm lost in a weeklong maze of fear and fatigue. I'll support myself, my family, and my work by setting clear boundaries and checking in early with people who can help me get clear on my direction and perspective on problems—before I feel the entire weight of the world. That way, neither my children nor I will have to suffer. And maybe work will be easier, too.

Sane Ways to
Create Strong Boundaries

১৯৯৯

1. *Write down your boundaries—the rules you set to show the world how you are to be treated.* Practice them. Learn to keep them. Stay away from people who do not honor your boundaries—bedtimes, off-limits discussion topics, or places and activities that are not acceptable to you. Inform first, but then disengage if necessary. Remember: boundary busters are not your friends. They can sabotage your turnaround.

2. *If you have people walking all over you, or notice that when someone around you is depressed you become depressed, or find yourself saying yes when you really want to say no, you probably are among the millions of people who could benefit from a thorough reading of the book* **Codependent No More** *by Melody Beattie.* It's a lifesaving guide on learning how to set boundaries and create healthier relationships. Anyone can benefit from

reading it but especially those of us who grew up with or have lived around active addiction.

3. ***Make a schedule.*** Post it. Stick to it to the degree that it supports you.

4. ***Go to bed early and get at least eight hours of sleep.*** Your sleep boundary is crucial. Unless there's an emergency or they're sick, do not let your children break this boundary. Turn on your answering machine so that someone calling you past your bedtime doesn't wake you up. Ask that they not call you past that time anymore. Further, most children simply do not get enough sleep. Make sure you are absolutely clear about bedtimes for your children. Put them in bed early. The time after they go to sleep is yours. For your sake, and theirs, make sure you get it.

5. ***If you're single, make your bedroom a sacred place for you and you alone.*** Single or married, you need one space that is just for you, even if it is just a corner of the bedroom.

6. ***Notice those who are good with their own boundaries.***
   Ask them to support you in living the same way. Also
   notice who respects and supports your boundaries.
   These are your friends.

7. ***After 9:00 PM postpone all emotional or highly charged
   discussions until the next day.*** Everything seems more
   intense late at night. And it's too hard to go to sleep
   after an intense conversation. At night, keep conversations short, and stick to sports, news, and weather.

8. ***When life seems out of hand either at work or with the
   children—money is short, time is short, and you're
   stressed—practice this mantra:*** With God's help I am
   big enough and strong enough to take care of myself
   and my children, and when I need human help, I don't
   hesitate to ask for it.

5

Make Better Decisions

The better our choices, the better our lives. Our lives show the world what choices we're making. When we are being decisive, take-charge family leaders, our self-respect grows, increasing the respect our children have for us. By watching us, our children learn to make better choices for themselves. When we put rules and order into our lives, we actually reduce the number of choices we have to make because we are creating routines and consistency. Doing the same thing over and over each day—waking up, meals, and bedtimes—brings safety and sanity into our lives. This consistency creates serenity for our loved ones and ourselves, especially when we are beginning a program of recovery or any other effort to turn around or create order in our lives.

THE PAIN STARTS HERE:

windowsill roulette

I am five or six years old. It's late. Mother and Daddy are in the den. He has threatened to kill her a hundred times. I am so afraid that he will do it this time that I am tinkling in my pants. This could be the time he really does it. Or maybe not. He threatens, slaps, and hits. I see this through a crack in the door, and then I run to my room.

I open the window, and I look down. I want to go get help. It is a long way to the ground. If I jump I will land in bushes and cut myself. But that isn't what scares me most. It is running through the night to Miss Mary Anne's house next door. It's just a few steps and down a little hill. But it is dark and scary. I will be waking up her family in the middle of the night.

Worst of all, if I go and tell them Daddy is killing Mother, he might kill all of us. So I go back and forth, back and forth on that windowsill. Go. Stay. Stay. Go. What's best? If I go and tell, the police will come, and everyone will know. Daddy will be so mad that if he can't kill her tonight, he'll do it later.

If I don't go, either he'll kill her or they'll finally stop fighting. Tomorrow morning they'll act like nothing happened, and I'll go to school and throw up. Somehow my brother will keep sleeping through all of it.

I hate making decisions. And I hate myself because I can't decide.

History Almost Repeats Itself:
Living the Pattern

I am fourteen or fifteen years old. Mother and I are in the middle of a huge fight in the carport. I am tired. Tired of going to school and falling asleep. Tired of failing chemistry. Tired of being a loser at school dances, hiding out and primping in the bathrooms. Tired of feeling sad all the time. Tired of never doing anything right. Tired of being too skinny, too stupid, too everything, but never being enough of anything.

I can't take it anymore, and I tell her that if she and Daddy don't get a divorce, I am moving in with my best friend and will not come back. I cannot live in this house anymore with the fighting and the screaming, the guns, knives, and being jarred awake by the sounds of glass breaking in the middle of the night. I tell her that if she is stupid enough to stay and have this crap happen to her, she can let it happen to her alone, because I am getting out. I have talked it over with my best friend's mother, and she says I can move in. I am dead serious. I have made the decision. And I have a plan.

A month or two later, Mother takes the first step to file for a divorce. Daddy is living in the cabin at the lake. My brother goes to live with him. I am left here with Mother. She accuses me of taking drugs, of having hickies (I've never even kissed a boy because I'm so afraid of them), of all kinds of things that I don't do. She hates her life right now, so she hates me, and it is nuts.

I live there for another two years, staying away from home as much as I can. I have no idea that the reason I feel like dying about three-quarters of the time is because I am depressed. Or that I am co-addicted to my parents—so insanely wrapped up in their manic ups and downs that I feel the same anger, rage, shame, and guilt they feel. I go to summer school again, so I can graduate at seventeen, a full year ahead of my class. My friends are surprised and angry when I tell them two weeks before school's out that I've decided to graduate early. But I do it. I move into a little shanty that slaves lived in before the Civil War. Daddy pays the rent.

With nothing better to do, I start college in my hometown three days after high school graduation.

Though I despise my father's alcoholism, in my late teens beer and wine become *convenience-store ready medication.* They are easily accessed relief for bad moods, and a dose of courage to cover the insecurities that have me holed up in bathrooms at dances and parties. I am always afraid I'll be asked on a date and always afraid I won't be asked.

I simultaneously work on the college newspaper and become its youngest editor in chief, take a full load of classes, hold down a part-time job selling newspaper advertising in a town fifty miles away, and cover football games and city council meetings for the local radio station—rushing everywhere I go. After two years of burying myself in work and school, I finally get the opportunity to leave my hometown for an internship with a United States senator. I leap at the chance and gleefully announce I won't be home again. I enroll at George Washington University (GWU) and keep working on Capitol Hill. At nineteen I become so overwhelmed by school, work, and my first real relationship that I escape what the school psychologist calls "an imminent breakdown" by taking on an even bigger challenge.

I leave college my junior year to dive headfirst into one of America's greatest legal adrenaline rushes—working on a presidential campaign. I deeply respect and trust Jimmy Carter. More than a year and a half before he announced his candidacy, I drove 120 miles round-trip several times to help put together fund-raising materials for his campaign. Two years later, as a full-time staffer, I take on high-stress assignments like driving hot-off-the-press brochures overnight from Atlanta to Chicago on the dare that I won't make State Street by dawn, taking scores of volunteers from Minnesota to campaign in Montana, and making all the transportation, entertainment, and other arrangements for 100 of Carter's best supporters invited to the 1976 Democratic National Convention. During that time, I run through the streets of New York City in the middle of the night with convention passes and special invitations. My last assignment is to help plan the election-eve party in Atlanta. I loved having a cause: get Jimmy Carter elected president of the United States. Busy with a world-class purpose, I am able to stuff those lifelong feelings of fear, shame, and inadequacy deep down inside until the campaign ends, and I find myself alone, back in school at GWU, so miserable that I can't concentrate well enough to read, much less study.

Working full-time at a public-relations firm and taking night classes, I trudge through downtown Washington in the dark in freezing cold weather, half hoping I'll get killed. Sometimes when I'm alone at the office, I lie down on the braided rug and cry for hours. I miss my campaign buddies and all the excitement, but I know that if I don't finish college now, I probably never will. So I try, alone, to outlast the devastating emotional withdrawal from the constant intensity generated by the campaign, and the loneliness I feel missing the 24/7 companionship of my friends. The shame about my inability to "buck up" is unbearable. So I do what good little addicts do: I stay in motion, drink, nearly overdose on sugar, and look for more ways to avoid my feelings.

Several months later when the hotshot public-relations firm I am working for is about to be sold, I jump at the chance to end that job and hide out in the home of a coworker, the first truly peaceful person I have ever known. As the nanny of her two children, I can finish the term at GWU while I get my bearings. I sublet my apartment, move in with this wonderful family, and promptly gain thirty-five pounds. Two months later, after a visit home for a friend's wedding, my best friend from my high school swim team helps me to engineer my next escape: move to Knoxville to finish college at the University of Tennessee (UT) and live with her and another teammate. She swears she's going to "get my fat butt in that UT pool and help swim it off."

I've been at UT for about four months when I finally make good on a two-year-old promise made to the school psychologist at GWU. I had sworn to him that when the presidential campaign ended and I settled down in school, I would find a professional counselor to help me figure out why I had been running so hard so fast for so many years.

My first appointment with a counselor in Knoxville is after a nightmare visit home for Christmas, when a stomach ulcer lands me in the hospital. Reacting to the ulcer medication and drinking heavily, I am unusually uninhibited and have a fling with an older guy. I don't go home some nights. As part of my Christmas present,

Mother pays for me to go to a campaign-staff reunion party in Washington. My friends work in the White House; I am a lowly college student. I feel so out of place there that I contemplate suicide, leave early, and become horribly sick at a friend's house where I'm staying. Nothing that a good shopping spree can't cure, I tell myself, so I blow what little money I have on clothes and don't make it through the first week back at school without having to call Daddy and beg him to cover checks for me. Asking for money always makes me feel extremely anxious. I can work up huge *angst* (toxic intensity) over being a giant burden—until I start drinking. Then I don't worry about it because the irony of buying beer with Daddy's money makes me laugh.

Over beer after beer I brag about my experiences in politics, dig myself into deeper trouble with school and money, and fantasize more about committing suicide.

So I start my therapeutic journey by drinking daily and beating myself up about my holiday exploits. A few weeks later, I test the patience of my therapist when I meet a slightly older student who works full-time and is impressed with my political experience. In a drunken confession I arm him with enough information about past boyfriends to keep our eighteen-month-long relationship intense, addictive, and abusive, making schoolwork and healing even more dull and difficult, because his tirades help me to feel as worthless as I know I am.

My therapist does her best to keep me focused on surviving and graduating in spite of my addictions to money mismanagement, work, alcohol, and this harddrinking, abusive man. At times I also binge on sugary foods, gaining and losing weight in fast cycles that include swimming mile after mile and obsessing into guilt-rich, calorie-burning anxiety attacks that require more alcohol for relief.

My favorite advisor praises my ability as a writer but adds a sad and shocking P.S.: "You leave a path of destruction wherever you go." Not entirely true, but true enough to sting, hurt, and push me to want to make some changes—like getting out of college as fast as I can.

I finally finish my course work, becoming the first member of our family to earn a college degree. In a bizarre graduation celebration, my parents and I have dinner together for the first time in almost ten years. Daddy has

Rusty Nails to drink and a pistol in his pocket (he never goes anywhere without at least one gun). Mother takes a few pictures, in which I look terrified and miserable. It is a fitting finish to my southern tour of colleges.

My choices stink, but I don't have any idea how to start making better ones. I just go back and forth a hundred times on stupid decisions, always afraid, welcoming the moment's relief I feel when someone else finally makes a choice for me.

THE TURNAROUND:

The House Was Talking

I t is a summer evening two years after my divorce, and it's been another in a long line of incredible weeks. As my significant other and I broke up Sunday night, the toilet overflowed, leaving a crescent-shaped stain on the kitchen ceiling. Water actually poured out of the light fixture. Just one more assault on this wonderful house, following last week's death of the oven. I could go through the litany of destruction here: from the kitchen floor trashed by a broken pipe in a late-season freeze, to the carbon monoxide–leaking furnace that was condemned by the fire department and sent me, fearful of carbon monoxide poisoning, to the hospital in the middle of the night, to the blowup of the rusted-out hot water heater, to the recently replaced pump for the downstairs toilet—and that's all been in the course of three months. Is God trying to tell us to get the hell out of this house while it's still standing, or to take the stand to stay and figure out how to fix it?

As I see it, we get out now, downsize, simplify, and embrace the reality that I am not a workaholic anymore and that I choose not to be addicted to my own adrenaline. I choose now to live a more peaceful life with less expense and more sanity.

As I sit here working today, a real estate agent comes to show the house. I hear the prospect say to the agent, "I would never want to be in a situation like this." I guess he means he'd never want to be in a house that needs so much work done on it and needs to be unloaded fast—even though I advertised it as a "fixer-upper."

I laugh. I think he has no idea about my situation: I have my health and two healthy children, and for the first time in my life I have real sanity, hope, energy, and passion. This house has been a deliverance place where I've experienced the rebirth of my soul, the rebirth of my relationships with my children, and the birth of my willingness to delve into the darkness of my past and let it go, making room for the light of this day.

In this house I've experienced the epiphany that comes with learning how to say no and the joy of learning how to live without the trappings I used to think defined me. This house has also been the birthplace of new business ventures, important relationships, the constant restructuring and maturing of my relationship with my mother—the list goes on and on.

I think to myself, "That guy should be so lucky as to be in a situation like this. The house may need repairs, but my foundation has never been stronger." There is a deep and abiding gratitude in this home. Gratitude for being able to laugh and not judge. Love unconditionally. Let go. Sit still and just be. Accept change. Create change. Make mistakes. Count my blessings. Cut my losses. Live instead of just exist.

READER/CUSTOMER CARE SURVEY

HEMG

We care about your opinions! Please take a moment to fill out our online Reader Survey at **http://survey.hcibooks.com**. As a **"THANK YOU"** you will receive a **VALUABLE INSTANT COUPON** towards future book purchases as well as a **SPECIAL GIFT** available only online! Or, you may mail this card back to us and we will send you a copy of our exciting catalog with your valuable coupon inside.

First Name	MI.	Last Name

Address		City

State	Zip	Email

1. Gender
- ☐ Female ☐ Male

2. Age
- ☐ 8 or younger
- ☐ 9-12   ☐ 13-16
- ☐ 17-20 ☐ 21-30
- ☐ 31+

3. Did you receive this book as a gift?
- ☐ Yes   ☐ No

4. Annual Household Income
- ☐ under $25,000
- ☐ $25,000 - $34,999
- ☐ $35,000 - $49,999
- ☐ $50,000 - $74,999
- ☐ over $75,000

5. What are the ages of the children living in your house?
- ☐ 0 - 14   ☐ 15+

6. Marital Status
- ☐ Single
- ☐ Married
- ☐ Divorced
- ☐ Widowed

Comments

_____

_____

_____

_____

BUSINESS REPLY MAIL

FIRST-CLASS MAIL PERMIT NO 45 DEERFIELD BEACH, FL

POSTAGE WILL BE PAID BY ADDRESSEE

Health Communications, Inc.
3201 SW 15th Street
Deerfield Beach FL 33442-9875

Say no. And say *Hell, no!*

Just last night my children recited the Serenity Prayer—God grant me the serenity to accept the things I cannot change, the courage to change the things I can, and the wisdom to know the difference—with me. At ages three and six those voices so sweet spoke words that have changed my life forever. What a gift that we learned this prayer and shared it here in this tree house–like home overlooking a creek-filled gully. That we took the time to learn and love under this safe, cool canopy of trees so green, so incredibly lush, the emeralds must be jealous.

It is, and is not, easy to leave this place.

I am more and more willing to make choices and take risks as I teach my children how to be brave and sensible at the same time. We are learning how to listen to our heads and our hearts. And I am seeing every day that it's a lot better to accept the consequences of my choices than it is to freeze in fear or confusion and have choices made for me.

❧

Sane Ways to
Make Better Choices

१५७७७०

1. *Allow yourself time to think and list all your options before making big decisions.* Have a conversation with a trusted, unbiased friend or mentor. You need to know you're not alone in the process. You're not asking someone else to make decisions for you. You're simply talking about all the options, so you can make the best choice.

2. *Make decisions when you're feeling calm and peaceful— not frustrated, overwhelmed, hungry, tired, or angry.*

3. *Rarely say yes in the moment. Say you will have to think about your answer.* Then take the time you need to get clear on your current and upcoming commitments. You want a reserve—a stockpile—of time, money, and energy for you and your family, and you're more likely to have a reserve if you don't overpromise or say yes in the

moment. Saying yes right away may please the person asking you to do something, but making good on a hasty commitment can lead to giving more than you really have, or debting. Overpromising—time, energy, money, or talents—is draining and depleting and ultimately makes us sick. (I know about this because I've done it so often. Now I rarely say yes in the moment to anything more than another cup of decaf coffee, or something equally as unimportant.) I used to hate to disappoint people with my no answer. Now I understand that when I overpromise, nobody wins, and I am usually the one who loses the most.

4. ***Remember you're making decisions for a family.*** If something doesn't work for your children—taking them to a meeting, grocery shopping, or anywhere else when you know they're too fussy or tired—it probably won't work for you.

5. ***When you're tired and overwhelmed, take the path of least resistance.*** Open a can of soup instead of trying to meet friends and their children for pizza or trying to

make a complicated dinner. Simplifying like this may seem boring. But remember, you're looking to lower intensity and stress.

6. ***Constantly seek ways to conserve your energy.*** Loosen your grip on the steering wheel a bit. You don't have to leave the house in perfect order. Bath toys can stay in the tub. Beds don't have to be made.

7. ***Make a list of three little things that annoy you, and change one of them this month.*** They are draining you—don't let them. For example, if you have a tear in your nightgown, just fix it. Or if all your cups have chips, buy a couple of new ones at a dollar store.

8. ***When faced with a tough decision, ask yourself, "Is this a sane, TurnAround Parent thing to do?"*** If the answer is no, don't do it. If you have trouble coming to an answer, call your check-in partner, sponsor, or a friend. Or ask yourself, "Would I want my children to do this someday?"

9. ***Lighten up.*** Abuse survivors, alcoholics, other addicts, and adult children of alcoholics can be intensely serious at times. If your fears stop you, learn to laugh at yourself and accept that there are no mistakes, only opportunities to learn new ways of doing things. A caring sponsor from your support group, a therapist, or a friend can help you find your sense of humor. Best of all, let your children help you find your sense of humor. Curl up on the sofa with them and read a silly book or watch an age-appropriate video that'll help you to laugh, too. Laughter really is great medicine. A good chuckle can change your whole day. You'll make better decisions when you stop taking everything so seriously.

10. ***When it comes to making any decision, be honest and clear on your real needs.*** Then get out of the problem and into the solution by clearly and honestly asking for what you need. If you think it will help to tell the other person why making a certain choice or request is important to you, tell him or her, but don't overexplain. Getting your needs met is a challenge if you've been in a depressed state for a long time. Practice

meeting your needs by asking for little things first—
the salt, a fresh pot of coffee, the seat you really want—
and asking will get easier. Then work your way up to
the bigger needs and wants: time off from work, a
raise. For some of us, it really does take practice and
tremendous courage to ask for what we need and want.
Be sure to acknowledge your own progress, and have
someone else acknowledge you, too, as you make
breakthroughs along the way.

6

Spend Your Precious Resources Wisely— Energy, Time, Money

When we live beyond our means, we set ourselves up for the relentless toxic intensity of not paying bills on time. We create fear and pain as we juggle what money we do have, paying some of our bills one month, others the next, wasting our money on high interest rates and late fees. Many of us attempt to stop the pain via drugs, alcohol, food (usually something sweet because we're missing the sweetness in life), sex, spending even more—whatever takes the pain away for the moment. The consequences of incurring this debt are staggering:

worry, insecurity, the constant sense of lack, the unending calls from bill collectors. Our children won't respect our disciplining them if we don't respect and discipline ourselves. How we spend—money, time, and energy—is a great way to set the example.

THE PAIN STARTS HERE:

the beginning of the "buy-highs"

The Jitney Jungle was our grocery store of choice when I was growing up. It had a great magazine section, filled with *MAD* magazine and lots of comic books—*Archie, Little Lotta, Richie Rich*. It also had the universal set-Mom-up-to-be-hit-on-for-junk counter right by the checkout.

After work, Mother would race home, put the maid and us into the car, "run" the maid home, stop by the vegetable stand, and then stop at the grocery store. The timing was a lot less than perfect. She was tired and was probably feeling guilty about being gone all day. We were hungry to see her—wild, whiny, needy.

It was a perfect setup. We wanted *her*. But because she didn't have a lot of energy to give, we decided to settle for *stuff*: comic books and stupid little toys like water pistols, jewelry sets, wooden airplanes, and bolo paddles. And we knew how to get them: tell Mother what an awful time we'd had with the maid. That we really needed to do something fun. That we'd been inside all day. That we were bored. That we never got to do anything. That we felt sad. *We learned early on how to play the victim to become the victor.*

Physically worn out by her job, emotionally exhausted from wondering when and what kind of shape Daddy would be in when he got home (cheerful, raging, sloppy drunk, hungry, demanding, violent, horny, or close to passing out), she was an easy mark. She hated to hear us whine, and the easiest known antidote was a cheap prize.

So we learned this great routine: be needy. Use guilt. Pitch a little fit. Stir up some drama. Get your adrenaline into it. You feel better when you get what you want, for a while anyway.

It was perfect. Mother could buy a moment of peace—we could buy a moment of control and fulfillment. It was a "buy-high," and I was soon addicted to it. And I believe Mother was soon addicted to letting me have it, even if the high didn't last a whole minute. Even if the connection was made by a comic book or Pixie Stix, we both got the fix we needed. Both of us winning and losing at the same time.

History Almost Repeats Itself: The Sand in the Oyster at PetSmart

It is your typical soccer-mom Saturday. The basketball game started at 8:00 AM. Gymnastics class was at 10:00. We've completed lunch and several missions. Next on the list: buy crickets for my son's lizard. We've made a pact in the car; just crickets, nothing else.

Kenny is tired. Raw. The game and the errands have

worn him out. I sense this as we go into PetSmart but figure I can get us in and out before an eruption. I still haven't learned that if a power play is brewing, it's best to load up and go home. Period. But I know Kenny's pet lizard is hungry. So we head to the cricket counter, and I ask our salesclerk to bag the bugs as quickly as possible. While we wait, we walk around and look at the fish. Sophie is enthralled. Kenny has on his shopper-radar face, eyes darting, looking for that one thing he can't live without.

I forget now whether it was a salamander or a frog, but Kenny is standing at the tall tank, asking for it. Asking for it. Asking for it. And I say, in my important voice, "No. We have an agreement." Perhaps I could have said, "You may use your allowance to buy it the next time we come," but I didn't. All he gets is no. And he is ready for action. His hands go around the tank, forehead against the glass, body tensed in a don't-even-try-to-move-me stance.

Sophie is with me. We pay for the crickets. As I walk toward Kenny, he makes another move, darting around the wall of fish food and past a row of empty aquariums.

He glues himself to the tank again, this time with his cheek plastered to the glass. He digs in his heels. So here I stand with a bag of crickets as I hold a tired three-year-old and watch a wrathful six-year-old fully wrapped around a fragile glass tank filled with semirare reptiles.

I've been working on my own parenting ideas—researching, reading, and talking with friends, my therapist, and people who teach workshops and classes on parenting. I know getting bent out of shape will only add to the insanity. I am so tempted to escape the discomfort of this moment by giving in and buying whatever creature it is that he wants. And I know I will only make matters worse if I do give in. I will set us both up for more of the same scream-till-you-get-what-you-want game. So I hand the crickets to Sophie and tell her to hold my hand. I tell Kenny this is his last chance to come peacefully. He digs in harder.

For better or for worse, I stay quiet, somehow restrain his arms as I pick him up and head quickly for the door. We are surrounded by glass. With Sophie wide-eyed and frightened, I haul Kenny out, holding him as close to me as I possibly can. He is kicking and screaming and using every bit of force a rage-fueled six-year-old can muster. It is and is not one of my finest moments.

Somehow we get to the car, and I tell Sophie to stand by the tire and not move. Getting the car unlocked with Kenny pounding on me is not easy. He breaks free, plants a full force soccer kick into my shin, and runs. I catch him and drag him, in a bear hug, until I can sit us down with my back against the car. I take a deep breath. He is wild. I tell him to take a deep breath. He bites my arm. I find the keys, stand up with him still in my grip, and open the door. I have a three-year-old to load into a car seat and a six-year-old to hold on to in the middle of a busy parking lot. Godly grace intervenes. Somehow I get them both in the car, Kenny still kicking. I am breathing. Remaining calm. Keeping my mouth shut to keep the drama from getting any worse. Praying.

When we get home I send Kenny to his room. He trashes it. I hear books hitting the floor. I see mayhem when I open the door. Calmly, I hand him a piece of paper and a pencil. I ask him, unemotionally, to write down ten things he's happy to have in his life. I ask him to clean his room. And I calmly walk out—stunned that even though I'm not a spanker, I didn't want to smack the ever-loving beans out of him.

Later that afternoon, when he has remade his bed and picked up his toys, he comes out. At the top of his gratitude list I see his pets, father, family, and farther down I see that he is glad to "live in a free 'contry.'" He is sad. Strong. And though I pray to stay in the moment, I suddenly imagine Kenny as an angry teenager, six feet tall and towering over me.

I've already called the counseling center to find a therapist for my son, who is mad as hell that I asked his dad to leave, madder still that his dad left the state, and even angrier that his dad's visits are few and far between. I've also resolved to do more than the research and counseling I'm already doing. I pray that the parenting workshop I've signed up for will help me to do a better job at mothering, refereeing, running interference, and inspiring great behavior.

It's an amazing time. My son's outburst is the sand in the oyster. It stirs things up and demands to be smoothed, polished, and treasured lest it irritate more. With each irritation, there's another layer of God's milky balm available to coat us all. Thank God I keep choosing balm instead of grit. And saying no instead of stringing one mixed-message buy-high after another. And most of all, I thank God that I am not drinking. That would be a Niagara Falls of kerosene dumped on this raging fire, the guarantee of insanity for all of us.

THE TURNAROUND:

Who Bought All This Stuff Anyway?

The children are in Florida with their dad. I am starting the massive task of packing up our household. Where did all this stuff come from? Who the heck was I when I bought this stupid dress, this garage sale piece of furniture, this set of Bloomingdale's dishes, this $150 cooking pot, this pair of bronze metallic shoes, this pile of sexy exercise leotards, this putrid color of eye shadow, and about half the other stuff around here? When did I first start having shopping blackouts?

Truly, I haven't gotten that buy-high I used to get in a long time. And I am grateful to have put behind me that urge to buy something I really can't afford. You know the feeling—you see something you think you just can't live without, and you get that sudden attachment to it. Then obsession kicks in, and you know you simply must have that black blazer because "it's a classic," "it just looks so good on you," and "you'll be really, really glad you have it someday."

I make no apologies to my past advertising agency employers for climbing on my antimaterialism soapbox to preach against the evils of trying to buy happiness. Heck, I used to write ads. And then I decided there was no joy in selling people stuff they didn't really need, that they were probably buying with money they didn't necessarily have ("Just say, 'Charge it!'"), to impress people who most likely didn't give a flying rat's fanny about their stuff and status.

So tonight, after packing, I watched a raccoon on my deck. And loved every minute of it. The best shows in life—sunsets, rainbows, birds building nests—are free. It's the acting out of our anger, frustration, and depression that costs us. Costs us when we shop compulsively, spend compulsively, overeat, or do anything else to deaden pain and try to compensate for that sinking sense of inadequacy.

It's much more satisfying to sit out under the stars than in a noisy restaurant, to share a store-bought pizza with a friend than to rush to a movie, a party, or some dress-up event that used to inspire a shopping trip for something new to wear. I am grateful to take a deep breath, watch that raccoon climb a tree and stare back at me, and then go to bed early enough to get my beauty sleep, so I can feel, as I say to my daughter, "pretty from the inside out."

Even though I am in the middle of a massive move, this Friday night at home is sane and functional. It feels good to know that, and even better to live it. It's a feeling money just can't buy.

Sane Ways to Manage Money

ᴄ᷍ᴀ᷍ᴠ᷍

1. *Whether you're rich or poor, do whatever you can to avoid debt.* Postponing payment for something by using credit cards, pay advances, or loans from friends or family is called unsecured debt because you take debt on by using only your signature as promise to repay. There is nothing you can "give back" if you have problems paying as agreed. Instead, you'll wreck your credit and be hounded until you pay. Secured debt is debt that has collateral behind it, such as a car or a house, which the lender could take if you don't keep up the payment schedule.

2. *At almost all costs, avoid incurring additional debt to pay off past debts.* Instead, work out repayment plans that don't leave you strapped for living expenses. Overpaying creates a sense of neediness and can ultimately lead to more overspending. A small payment is better than no payment. Creditors will work with you

if you make a plan, stick to it as best you can, and stay in touch. There is an excellent, easy-to-read book by Jerrold Mundis that includes a great plan for getting out of debt: *How to Get Out of Debt, Stay Out of Debt, and Live Prosperously*. Another good book is *Money Drunk, Money Sober* by Julia Cameron and Mark Bryan.

3. **REMEMBER THIS:** *Debt can ultimately make you sick with anxiety if the bills come due and the money isn't there.* Think about it before you spend money when you're low on cash or savings. If you want to go into debt or overspend for something you can live without, try living without it a little while longer.

4. *If you have a problem with money management, find a Debtors Anonymous group immediately.* This is a twelve-step program based on the principles of Alcoholics Anonymous. To find the group nearest you, go to the website www.debtorsanonymous.org, call 1-781-453-2743, or check your local directory. Your local Consumer Credit Counseling Service (CCCS) is another good resource. CCCS helps with debt consolidation and negotiating payment plans with your creditors. Being

buried by a mountain of debt can make life miserable. With help from these resources, becoming debt-free is a possibility. The important thing is to ask for help.

5. *Debtors Anonymous members work to help each other "give up unrealistic expectations that there will be funds available in the future to cover expenses today."* In other words, don't make commitments based on money you don't have.

6. *Get into reality about money.* Reality is actually manageable. Get into the habit of knowing how much money you have in cash, savings, and your checkbook. This is invaluable for chronic money mismanagers. If you have to go on a cash-only basis (no checks or debit cards) for a while to stop chronic bounced-check fees and other costly bank charges, do so. Use money orders to pay bills, so you don't walk around with—and risk losing—a lot of cash.

7. *Realize that for some people, getting and spending money is just as big a high as using drugs.* If you get a buy-high, call Debtors Anonymous today.

8. *Start by having a spending plan for* **today.** Write down every penny you spend for one month to see where your slippery places are.

9. *Find ways to bring yourself comfort that do not involve spending money.* Hot baths. Walks. Talking to friends on the phone. Going to the park. Reading for fun.

10. **HOLD THIS THOUGHT:** *Saving money isn't denying yourself the use of money now. Saving money is actually another form of self-care.*

7

Attract Healthy Relationships

If you believe you are precious, you will not allow someone to treat you as if you are not. If you have a daughter, and she sees you abused, she'll think that's how women are treated by men. If you have a son, and he sees you abused, he'll think that's how men treat women or how spouses treat each other in general. This is life-and-death important. The old saying, "What children see, they learn. What they learn, they practice. What they practice, they become," doesn't have to be true. If you grew up in a home where people didn't respect one another, forgive that wound and vow to make a difference today. First, respect yourself. Then follow the good old Golden Rule: Treat others as you would have them treat you.

THE PAIN STARTS HERE:

what does a normal relationship look like, anyway?

I am eight years old. It's dark, and I am outside with my best friend, Ellen, and her neighbor Robert. There are others, but we are the only three who matter. Ellen is yelling at me, calling me a chicken. She is climbing the ladder to the tower, and I am afraid to go up. I hate heights, and she is yelling at me about being a big, stupid baby chicken.

Mother doesn't like Ellen but lets me play with her anyway. I can't wait to go to her house. She is wild, smart, and scary. And I need to be with her. She calls me names and makes fun of me because I am so skinny. She yells at her mother and calls her mother a bitch. We are just little girls, but nobody stops her.

We spend a lot of money on Saturdays while our mothers are at work. Her mom works at the store where we can go in and get all the comic books and candy we want, and if anyone tries to stop us, Ellen will yell at them. On Friday nights we stay up late and watch *The Twilight Zone,* and it scares me half to death. We sit in the dark of their den and eat popcorn until I can finally get up to crawl into the other twin bed in her room and read comic books for hours while she sleeps.

She might wake me up in the middle of the night to sneak out of the house, or we might wake up and call people to ask them if their refrigerators are running. We can pretty much do whatever we want, and it is a scary feeling, yet wonderful at the same time, until she hits her mother, yells at her grandmother, and yells at me. But I don't care. I gossip about her. She finds out about it and gets really mad. Then we are not best friends anymore, but we end up back together again because she needs someone to yell at, and I don't mind. And even if she's yelling at me and calling me names and hitting her mother, I would rather be at her house with her yelling at me than at my house with Daddy hitting Mother. I'd rather be anywhere than my house.

History Almost Repeats Itself: Do I Want a Partner or Another Critical Parent?

He is strong and handsome and so, so smart. I can't believe how wonderful it is that God has put us together. We are on our way back from a weekend at the lake home of some of our best friends, and he invites me to drive his new car. I am a little bit afraid but say I will do it. The minute I get behind the wheel I tense up. He has a certain way he drives when he's in a hurry. He weaves in and out of traffic at a few miles above the speed limit, and I am open to learning how he does it. This is the most intimate relationship I have ever had in my life, and I am willing to accept that maybe in the past I was unwilling to learn another way to do things from the men I have dated—and especially the man I married. So I give it a try, and it is horrible. I am afraid to drive this fast. I don't like darting in and out of traffic. His corrections are constant.

I finally cannot stand the running commentary any longer, so I tell him I want to pull over and let him drive, but I let him persuade me to continue. By the time we get to the restaurant where I am meeting a friend for dinner, I am so wound up I can barely breathe. If I were still drinking, this would be a prime time to slam down two beers really fast to get rid of the overwhelming anxiety. I haven't felt anxiety like this in years.

My friend, Frances, is concerned. I say that it's just me learning how to accept constructive criticism and how to be taught something by a man. The excuses pile up, and I finally settle down and blow past the red flags and the feelings I fling out like skeet on a shooting range.

A couple of months after the children get home from a long summer visit with their dad, I realize that I can't take the criticism and intensity anymore. I absolutely do not want my precious children around someone so dramatic as he is in his nerve-racking pursuit of perfection. So I end the relationship and pray he'll go away. Mercifully, he does.

Months later I am on that same highway, at about the same time of the day, as I return from taking the children to their father's. An anxiety attack wells up in my chest, and I think it's because I'm listening to a self-help tape about addictions and abuse. And it is partly the tape. But it is also partly that I remember what was going on the last time I was on this road. The criticism. The fear. The not getting it right. And I remember another night with this same man on the same road when he yelled at me about my children and how I was not disciplining them properly.

I am happy in this moment to be alone with the angst, the fear, the sadness, the gratitude, and the hope. There is no room in my life for that kind of stress and criticism ever again. I am ready to receive nurture and to be nurturing and patient. And I have the ability now—thank God—to recognize red flags and toxic intensity, and to walk, run, or drive away as soon as I feel the first twinge of toxicity.

About a week after these revelations, I thank God that my children's exposure to this man was limited to a half-dozen "family dates," and that if he was angry during those times, his anger was directed toward me. I also called Mother to ask her if she had noticed anything strange about Daddy when she was dating him. In a moment of genuine connection and clarity, she said that Daddy had been very impatient and acted irrationally several times while they were dating. I asked her why she didn't break off the relationship, what compelled her to go on and marry someone known to have such a turbulent side to his personality. She said she knew, on some level, that she was making a mistake, but her fear of not marrying him, not having him and his family as support when she was so alone and new to Daddy's hometown, was great enough to overrule that inner suspicion. During that conversation, Mother and I talked woman-to-woman about men, paying attention to red flags, and ending relationships. We reached a deeper level of understanding each other as a result of that conversation, and I am grateful to have had the opportunity to connect with her.

I Am as Gentle in My Relationship with Myself as I Am in My Relationship with My Children

On Sunday night I locked myself out of the house. On Monday I lost my calendar. The rain of rage I poured upon myself was forceful enough to make deep ruts in baked earth. Monday evening, midway through a support-group meeting where the topic was anger, I had an epiphany: If either of my children had locked the door or lost my calendar, I would never have yelled at them the way I yelled at myself. I would have said instead, "Well, let's see what we can do to get back in the house," or about the calendar, "It'll turn up." I would have laughed about it. I would have been kind. And if I had been angry, I would have let go of it fast. After all, the lockout and the lost calendar were unintentional.

Beyond that, if anyone, *anyone*, ever said things to my

children that I was thinking about myself, I would be all over the criticizer in a hurry. I would never, ever allow anyone to say, "You moron, how could you have walked out without the key?" or "You always have your calendar. How could you be so irresponsible?" or "Do you know it'll probably cost fifty dollars to get the locksmith out here? That's coming out of your hide."

I wouldn't let anyone say those things to my children, but I did say them to myself. As trite as it may sound, I promise that I will not say them to the child in me any more than I would allow someone else to say them to my children. I deserve the same amount of kindness I would show toward my children.

It's almost as though I've decided to take the wedding vows with myself: "I promise to love, honor, and cherish *me*." It sounds silly, I know. But maybe if we all took those vows to love, honor, and cherish ourselves first, there wouldn't be so many broken homes, so much drama, so many abused children, so much addiction and toxic intensity. After all, anyone who really loves you, and is healthy emotionally, wants you to take great care of yourself. If they're healthy, they are attracted to you in the first place *because* you take great care of yourself.

So I take the vow to myself. And I don't care if it does sound corny. You can throw the rice now. Just not too hard.

Relationships: Sane Ways to Protect Yourself and Your Family, Especially When Dating

‹⁂›

1. **RED ALERT:** *If you are afraid for your safety in a relationship, call your local battered women's shelter for advice right away.* Do not wait. It is child abuse for your children to witness someone being abusive toward you. Further, if someone is abusive toward you, he or she may start abusing your children. This is definitely not a risk worth taking. If you are afraid for your safety or that of your children, call the women's shelter the first minute you are safely away from the person who is or could be abusing you. If there's not a local number, call the **24-hour National Domestic Violence Hotline at 1-800-799-SAFE (7233) (TDD 1-800-787-3224)**.

2. **RED ALERT:** *If a person you're seeing drinks or rages, you and your children do not need to spend time around him or her.* Even if the negative behavior isn't

directed toward you right now, someday his or her
drinking, anger, or both may threaten your recovery
and jeopardize the safety and sobriety of your children.
If you wonder whether or not this person is abusive,
choose a safe time when you're alone to call **Prevent
Child Abuse America at 312-663-3520** and describe
the behavior of the person in question. That's a safe
way to get an outside opinion.

3. *Your first priority is yourself and your children.* Get
   your relationship with yourself and your children rock
   solid before you think about dating. If you're new to
   recovery and recently divorced (it's amazing how often
   I see that combination in support-group meetings), it's
   especially important to wait a year to start dating.
   Otherwise, it's too easy to get distracted from your
   own needs and the needs of your children.

4. *If you would be scared to leave your two-year-old with
   a potential date, don't go out with that person.* Further,
   keep your children out of your dating life. Only allow a
   date to meet them after you've been out together at

least ten times over at least two months. Really check someone out well before you expose your children to him or her. It's too easy for children to get attached and start fantasizing about having this person as their father or mother, for this person to fall in love with your children and be disappointed about not seeing them again if you break up, or worst of all, to bring a child abuser into your home.

5. ***If someone you're already dating does meet your children, watch his or her behavior.*** If he or she doesn't like your children or is irritable around them, leave the relationship. Your children are your first priority. If a person has hostile feelings toward your children now, the hostility is likely to get worse if you marry. You do not want your children around negativity and a potentially abusive situation.

6. ***Think of yourself as precious and sacred, and never allow anyone to treat you as if you're not.*** You deserve to feel loved and to be cherished. Remember, your children are always learning from you. If they see you treat

yourself with respect and see that you are treated well by others, they will be less likely to end up in undesirable relationships.

7. ***Wait until you're healthy to think about dating, or else you'll attract an unhealthy person into your life.*** This is another one of those truths that I believe to be a law of the universe: you will attract someone who is at your own level of well-being.

8. ***Dating is an opportunity to set and live by your own boundaries and standards.*** Your morals, choice of friends, and sense of self-worth speak volumes to your children. Keep the highest standards as you date, and your children will be much more likely to do the same.

9. ***Dating toxic people is not an option. If someone is not good for you, you do not belong together.*** Remember this law: if dating him or her makes you feel anxiety, fear, or less than good about yourself, or being with him or her makes you think about drinking or using drugs, stop dating that person.

10. ***You are too precious to be anyone's drug of choice.*** You can tell if someone's "using" you. If you have the sense that you're being used, detach as quickly as possible. If you need help ending such a relationship, call your local women's shelter, your counselor, your pastor—someone who can guide you through leaving the relationship.

11. ***If you think you may be in a verbally abusive relationship, read the book* The Verbally Abusive Relationship *by Patricia Evans.*** This easy-to-read book is full of examples that will help you recognize whether or not you are being abused. It will give you clear-cut actions to take and the tools you need.

8

Avoid
Toxic Intensity

Toxic intensity—self-induced anxiety—is addictive. If there is a high level of toxic intensity in your home, your children are likely to try to recreate it themselves with self-destructive behaviors. People recreate what they know from childhood because, even if it is bad, it is what they know, and people find comfort in the known. If your children hear arguing and verbal abuse, they become accustomed to it, and when they get into relationships of any kind (friendships, romantic relationships, work), they may attract someone who is toxic for them, and then not even know they're being abused or abusing others until the pain almost kills them. Toxic intensity can be created with violence, addiction, gossip, abuse, money mismanagement, rushing, obsessive thinking, overwork, or any other destructive, compulsive behavior. Being addicted to toxic intensity is a challenging, adrenaline-filled habit. Breaking this addiction takes a lot of work in setting and keeping boundaries, and in learning how to create and love peaceful times.

THE PAIN STARTS HERE:

he took my puppy and shot at us

Daddy carried a pistol wherever he went. He kept it in his pocket. He also kept one under the front seat of his car or in the glove compartment. Usually there was a shotgun in the trunk, too. He loved guns, hunting, drinking, and messing with his bird dogs. He loved the big, old lockbox on the back of his truck where he kept his guns and hunting stuff. He would send Mother outside late at night when he would get home from hunting and make her go get the dead birds and other game out of the truck to clean it for cooking or freezing. She was always afraid she would accidentally shoot herself with one of those guns.

One night Daddy hid a big live snake in that lockbox, so she would find it. I don't know how she lived through that. I don't even like to think how horrible it must have been for her to try to hold a flashlight so she could dig out those birds and then suddenly find her hand on a cold, coiled snake, especially since Mother is terrified of snakes.

He was a mean bastard sometimes. One night he decided he was going to take my Scottie puppy, Fala, away with him, so he could show my new puppy to his friends. He yanked that little dog up by the scruff of his neck and tore out of the house. Daddy tossed him into his car and drove away, with me crying and screaming at the top of my lungs. I was scared to death he would kill Fala; just slice him open like the quails and doves he gutted in the utility room sink. Mother got me and took me in her car after him. I don't know where my brother was—maybe at a friend's spending the night.

Mother knew where Daddy was going. We got there a couple of minutes after he did. She ran into the house and grabbed my puppy and jumped back into her car. As we drove off, he *shot* at us. *Shot at us with a gun. With real bullets.* None of them hit us or the car. I was crying on the floorboard, holding little Fala. Mother was shaking. I don't think Daddy came home that night. I just wished that he would die. For the millionth time, I just wished that he would die. How could this be the same person who'd taken us to Atlanta to buy the puppy a week before? How could he not even apologize for this insanity the next day, or ever?[1]

History Almost Repeats Itself:
If I Can Get Married, I Must Be Normal

Daddy died suddenly of complications from his alcoholism and diabetes on Thanksgiving Day 1981. A couple of days after his funeral, I learned that I had landed a great job. During the four years that I kept that job, I became a master at juggling credit cards, planning perfect parties, and drinking tirelessly. I was also a self-redeeming choir member at a beautiful Episcopal church. Some Sunday mornings I showed up for choir so hungover I almost threw up at the communion rail.

Once, as a bridesmaid, I walked down the aisle with a chinful of stitches. Totally trashed after the bachelorette party I'd thrown, I got pulled down the steps by my 100-pound golden retriever. "If you hadn't been so drunk, you'd probably have broken your back," the doctor said as he prescribed the back brace I'd wear for the next five months. The stitches came out a few days later, but the back trouble stayed with me for years. Of course, if I hadn't been so drunk, I probably wouldn't have been in such a mess in the first place, but I wouldn't admit to that drinking-causes-accidents connection. Alcoholism is like that.

When I was thirty, I added prescription painkillers to the mix after I had ripped my shoulder muscles unloading pumpkins for my church's youth group. The high school kids had asked me to be one of their advisors. They probably identified with me because I was about their same age—emotionally.

The painkillers complemented the martinis and beer chasers that numbed my shoulder pain but did nothing to stop the pain of being dumped by the dashing young millionaire I was hoping to marry. He probably ended the relationship because I'd acted out my insecurities so irrationally when I was laid off from my job. I was also totally uptight about the possibility of having to expose my mountain of debt. I couldn't let him know I was less than perfect. Even though I'd landed a better job within a week of being laid off, the cover-up about my finances and resulting panicky behaviors killed the relationship.

It was during this intensely painful, gin-soaked time that I managed to become engaged to a handsome artist—less than two months after our first date!

Reserved and talented, Bill was the exact opposite of the ego-driven, BMW-driving rich boys I had dated for years. When we were married just five months later, my mother thanked God that her friends could no longer wonder if I were an old-maid lesbian. She thought I was finally doing something normal. She didn't know I had a serious champagne buzz going as I walked down the aisle, or that later that night I could have broken my neck when, ripped on wine, I climbed on a wobbly stool at 4:00 AM and commanded my new husband to leave me alone while I changed a lightbulb on our tiny front porch.

When he moved into my house, where I earned 95 percent of our income and had 100 percent say in what happened, Bill got whammed full force by my issues of control and perfectionism. Then there was the expectation—which he had fueled—that he would have a sudden surge of success. This expectation was accompanied by big baggage: my lifetime of unmet needs for love and security. I think more than anything, Bill wanted some peace and quiet and a place to paint. He wanted to get on with his dream career of being a successful illustrator.

The glow of our brief courtship and beautiful wedding lasted almost a year. Then the truth of who we were started settling in: angry, driven alcoholic/workaholic (me) meets peaceful artist (Bill, age 29) who now shares his belief that all illustrators must be in their forties before achieving financial success. Waves of negative intensity, created by my overspending, attempts to control everything, debting, work addiction, codependency, immaturity, and alcohol abuse jolted through our marriage. I was so desperate to have a baby before "my eggs were out-of-date" that I turned myself into a work machine to pass the time until a few months past our first anniversary—just the right moment, I thought, to get pregnant.

Blessedly fertile, I never felt better in my life than when I was pregnant. Maybe it was because I couldn't drink. Maybe it was because it was so exciting to grow a baby at the same time I earned so much money. I worked myself so hard that I didn't take a full day away from clients either of the two times I gave birth. I talked with clients while I was in labor and within hours after both Kenny and Sophie were born.

As if I could control absolutely everything in the world, I even had both children on their respective due dates, which also happened to fall on weekends. I fought to avoid medication during delivery both times, knowing that I could get back to work faster if I didn't have to wait for an epidural to wear off. My compulsive spending and money mismanagement—buying new baby furniture, remodeling the house, hiring baby nurses when we couldn't afford them—left me little choice but to grab the phone and start adding up billable hours again between sitz baths and breast-feedings.

One thing I couldn't control was Mother's health. About ten days before Kenny was born, Mother was stricken with a rare disease that left her partially paralyzed. All her plans of coming to help with the baby were forgotten. Instead, I prayed she'd live to see her grandson. It was intensely emotional to visit her in the hospital knowing that I was days away from giving birth.

We were thrilled to learn that she would survive what was called a mild case of Guillain-Barré syndrome, a noncontagious viral infection with symptoms similar to those of multiple sclerosis. But it didn't seem real to see this active, powerful woman in a wheelchair for the first time on the same day she met her namesake grandson. As the months went by, her condition improved. She walked, though not well, and began to drive again.

Five years and another baby later, I knew my marriage would not make it. I didn't know that the main reason it wouldn't survive was because of my acting out the years of growing up in such insanity by living my life with full-force intensity. As I eased into my father's footsteps as an alcoholic, and my mother's footsteps as a codependent, I was hell-bent to control everything and everyone but myself. I couldn't tolerate what Bill and I had become: bitter, resentful, unloved and unloving people who adored our children but couldn't figure out how to grow up fast enough to save our marriage.

Divorce leads to introspection for most people. For an intensity addict, it leads to a full-scale self-dissection. For this intensity addict, I thank God daily that the disruption and destruction of my divorce ultimately resulted in a full-scale turnaround.

Losing the Stuff, Gaining My Life

Mother came to help a little during the days after Bill left. She offered no help, though, because most of the time she criticized my every move and told me that I was insane. I think my divorce must have brought up a lot of unresolved sadness about her own divorce from Daddy. All I knew then was that her words hurt and made me even more afraid, more depressed. So I asked her to leave. Several weeks later I was broken enough to finally take my seat at a support-group meeting for families and friends of alcoholics, and I joined a heavy-duty therapy program.

I refused to talk to Mother until I felt strong enough to hang up the phone whenever she started criticizing me. And I began putting my life back together by admitting I was powerless over the effects of my father's alcoholism and my own compulsive behaviors. Ultimately, I admitted to my own alcoholism. With God's help and by working a solid recovery program, I continue not to drink, one day at a time.

Turning my little family and myself toward a better place took working double-time in recovery and counseling and in an in-depth study of parenting that included a year of working with a parenting expert. I plunged into this new phase of life as feverishly as I had plunged into most everything else. But this time I was taking a far healthier plunge. And the results were profound: I got healthier in every way. My children were happier.

Over the next seven years I spent hundreds of hours and thousands of dollars working with family therapists to help me and my children learn how to handle our anger. In the beginning, my hardest task was accepting reality—the reality that I needed new skills to survive, new ways to live.

In addition to therapy, parenting workshops, and support groups, I spent hours in prayer, meditation, and journaling, on top of hours of listening to suggestions from advisors and mentors. I listened to self-help tape after self-help tape and memorized prayer after prayer, so I'd have something to replace the negative thoughts about myself that had crippled me for so many years.

I did the recovery work recommended by several self-help programs, studied the Bible, practically memorizing the book of Proverbs, and went on the antidepressant Zoloft for a while. This medication was a lifesaver that helped clear my brain, so I could absorb new information and adopt new behaviors. I learned how to turn my love of nature and reading into connecting points with my children. And I constantly reminded myself that in the face of fear, I could trust God and use my new tools to care for myself instead of isolating myself and falling back on spending, drinking, overworking, or other destructive, intensity-evoking diversions.

These efforts to improve myself might have been just as compulsive as my earlier efforts to destroy myself. But the results were visible in the way my little family became more and more loving, more and more functional. And I now had sane and loving people to check in with along the way, people who knew how to recognize and let me know when I was sounding "a little too out there." The rewards of the work were priceless. I gained the ultimate tool for serenity: being able to accept that I wasn't perfect.

Never could be. That acceptance of myself was the key to getting better.

As the smoke cleared after the divorce, I also joined a recovery program that helps people with compulsive debting, spending, and underearning. Thankfully, I had achieved some degree of self-acceptance when the reality hit that during the last two years of my marriage, I angrily spent my way into $52,837 worth of personal, unsecured debt. More than $17,000 of that I owed the Internal Revenue Service.

To help liquidate the debt, I held garage sales, selling thousands of dollars' worth of personal belongings for nickels on the dollar. Sometimes the children were there and saw baby furniture and other familiar comforts being hauled away. They learned early on to say, "Don't cry over anything that can't cry over you."

I'll never forget the look on my son's face when, in a cold, pouring rain, I auctioned off a huge truckload of sofas, armoires, dining-room furniture, and treasure-filled boxes—including my wedding gown and family heirlooms—to pay the debt on storage fees and cover some living expenses. Kenny was looking at me to know how to react. If I could face change with serenity and acceptance, maybe he could, too. My smile grew as my load was lightened and packed into a waiting truck. He smiled, too. His smile taught me a huge lesson. It was a peace that "passes all understanding." It was visual affirmation of a healthy "child see, child do" moment that marked the beginning of a new way of life filled with greater peace and less stuff.

Sane Ways to Avoid
Toxic Intensity

∽≈∾

1. *If your life is filled with anxiety—drama over relationships, tension about money, stress about work and
   other major issues, consequences of drinking or using
   drugs—stop trying to handle it all on your own.* Get
   help from a mental health professional, and find an
   appropriate twelve-step support group, be it Al-Anon
   for friends and family members of alcoholics, CODA
   for people who struggle with issues of codependence,
   Alcoholics Anonymous, Narcotics Anonymous, or other
   groups that deal with your concerns. There are support
   groups for everything from love and relationship addiction to overeating to emotions to money mismanagement. Do not suffer. If you don't have money for
   therapy, simply go to the twelve-step program best
   suited for you. These programs are free. You will find
   help there. It's likely that the longer you suffer, the
   greater the effects of your problem.[2]

2. *If you are the parent of young children, it is especially crucial that you get help with whatever problem is causing your anxiety.* Your children are literally immersed in and surrounded by whatever you are going through because children don't have the ability to block out the feelings of those around them the way adults do. Though your children may not seem aware of your tension, the feelings they are absorbing are bound to have an effect in acting out behavior, illness, or problems at preschool or school. Also, these problems are likely to reappear as your children hit puberty. If anxiety is around children, they will probably act it out one way or another.

3. *Replace obsessive thoughts—about boyfriends, money problems, wanting a drink, being angry—with a quiet mantra.* You'll be a lot less likely to act out. These are my mantras: I trust you, God. I trust you, God; Thank you, God. Thank you, God; or this new twist on an old chant, Even in the midst of chaos, all is well. All is well. All shall be well.

4. *Get yourself to a peaceful place and carve out thirty minutes of nonintense, no-instruction-giving, no-demands quiet time with your children before they go to bed.* If you can't devote thirty minutes, do as much as you can. Five minutes is better than nothing. The point is just to have some quiet time to connect, to really be with your children, when there are no distractions. You want to let them know how important they are to you; you want them to experience you as a calm and centered adult.

5. *Take a couple of minutes of quiet time for yourself in your car before you pick up your children from school or day care.* Take this time to breathe deeply, get centered, and put the stresses of your day behind you, so your time with them is really your time with them.

6. *If a situation with someone who evokes anxiety in you becomes heated, try to de-escalate the situation by talking slowly and softly and by staying calm.* If this kind of thing occurs frequently, consider changing your life, so you do not have to deal with this person so often. If

you must see a person such as this because of work, find someone who can help you either desensitize yourself to him or her, or limit your exposure to the person. Perhaps you can imagine him or her as a little child and, thereby, not feel so threatened by this person. All of this takes work, and I do not want to oversimplify or seemingly underestimate its importance.

7. *If you are attracted to someone who is toxic to you, get help immediately.* Talk to someone in a twelve-step group for relationship addicts. If you are healthy you will not be attracted to those who are toxic; you will want to stay away from them. Get help with this as soon as possible, because if you are attracted to one person who is toxic, it is likely that you'll be attracted to another person who is toxic unless you get help through therapy, through work with your minister or spiritual counselor, or by working with someone who has many years of recovery in twelve-step work.

8. *In a toxic situation, use your eyelids.* Sometimes when the world is too much—even while someone is talking

to you—just close your eyes, even if it's just for a split second. Doing this affirms to you that you do have some power over how much input is coming at you.

9. ***If you are surrounded by toxicity, practice self-care as best you can.*** Take a long, hot bath in a quiet bathroom, with bath salts and peaceful music, at least twice a week. A healing bath like this is best done after children have gone to bed. Use these baths and other ways to recharge yourself: drink a cup of herbal tea, write in your journal, sit for a while with your cat on your lap. The point is to find something peaceful and quiet that helps you to get to a positive place to help counteract the toxicity.

10. ***Pray the Serenity Prayer several times a day.*** Some days I have said it a hundred times or more. Say it over and over: God, grant me the serenity to accept the things I cannot change, courage to change the things I can, and wisdom to know the difference.

11. ***Remember that families, especially families where there are children younger than ten, operate best when they***

do just one or two big things in a day. For example, soccer and a birthday party may be okay, but soccer, a birthday party, and bowling will probably cause a meltdown. Also, monitor everyone's sugar consumption. Too much sugar—doughnuts, a soft drink, and no protein for several hours—is a recipe for disaster in most children, especially those who are already tired or overstimulated by too much activity. Add a toxic adult to wired and tired children, and you have the opportunity for a lot of drama and hurt feelings.

12. ***Teach your children the value of silence—how to ride in a car for a while or be somewhere without conversation.*** This will help them avoid discomfort when no one is talking and avoid the temptation to say something that is best not said.

9

Practice Peace: Rushing Is Abusive

Rushing is another way to create toxic intensity and feed an addiction to adrenaline. Intensity creates anxiety. Anxiety creates pain and the need to soothe the pain by acting out with alcohol, money, drugs, sex, food, or other compulsive behaviors. Acting out usually creates more problems, resulting in greater intensity and more anxiety, addiction, and abuse. One of the best ways to lower intensity is to stop rushing. Rushed children think they're doing something wrong if they can't get dressed, complete homework, or handle household chores as fast as adults can. When we rush our children, we are telling them that they are too slow and that they aren't good enough to keep up. If we don't want them to become accustomed to the abuse of being rushed and to have the "You're not good/fast/smart enough" message with them for the rest of their lives, we must slow our lives down a little to adjust to their pace and give them the positive experience of not being pushed or rushed. It may take a while. Patience—and getting an earlier start on the day—is the key.

THE PAIN STARTS HERE:

Daddy's golden death machine

I went to a support-group meeting where one of the regulars talked about faith, feeling safe, and having a sense of the God-conscience—

about living your life as a prayer. This man said he always felt safest when his dad picked him up and he was riding beside his father on the front seat of their big, old car. He described their trips together, the closeness they felt. The more he talked, the closer I came to falling apart. A pain washed over me that made me cry. I had an overwhelming sense of being totally out of control.

It took me a few minutes to realize why the pain had come; I was remembering that the times I was on the front seat with my dad were some of the times I felt the most frightened. I was most terrified that my daddy, dosed up on that stinky Early Times bourbon and "Co-Cola," driving that 427-horsepower Grand Prix, and flying down country roads with us bouncing around like popcorn popping would finally just take off and I would fly through a windshield or out a window of that golden death machine, slam into something, and die— this all because we had to be somewhere by 6:30, all because he got tied up at the office. All because we got stuck behind a pulpwood truck and couldn't pass it. All because I had to stop and go to the bathroom on the way out here. All because . . .

Whatever the reason, there was no reasoning behind his rush and craziness surrounding us and cars. There was, for me, only fear as we sat in that gold car and waited for him to come out of the Veterans of Foreign War (VFW) post where he'd stop to buy liquor and park the car in a hurry and so near the edge of a rock quarry we knew we'd fall out if we opened the door. Or there was the fear that if we didn't keep our weight on the far side of the car, it would slide into the quarry and we'd drown. It seemed that when I was with him, there was only and always fear. Fear he'd come out drunk and accidentally throw the car in reverse and plunge the whole shooting match into the quarry.

Whatever. Wherever. Time was always short. We were always eating up "his" time with needing to go to the bathroom or wanting something to eat or drink. I felt like I couldn't get small enough fast enough.

I remembered all of that at the support group meeting and came home and cried until I was all cried out. I was upset until I wrote in my journal that fathers need to treat their children as though they are the most precious, amazing beings they'll ever see. Fathers need to hold their children as though they are fragile and play with them gently. They need to be big and strong for their children, and never frighten them with games that are too rough or words that are scary. They need to be there, present, fully aware of what is happening, what is said, and ways their behavior can absolutely devastate a child.

Fast cars, big guns, sharp knives, empty boxes of shotgun shells, the smells of gun oil and bourbon. The thought of those smells still makes my stomach hurt. The thought of bouncing around in that car, in the bucket seat next to Daddy, watching his diamond ring glisten as we speed through the darkness, watching the cigarette glow hotter as he takes a long drag on it—these remembrances are all too much like being on a break-your-neck roller coaster in the pitch-black dark, even if it is thirty-five years later.

History Almost Repeats Itself:
The Saturday-Morning-Kids-Are-Gone-
I'm-in-a-Hurry-to-Move Crazies

I am feeling a surge of anxious energy that makes this a dangerous moment. Maybe you know how that feels. You're a bit rested, revved up, and ready to take on the world. And right now this wild energy is pulsing through me like jet fuel on fire. I feel compulsive, a little crazy, and ready to blast out in a million different directions: work, calling the children at their dad's in Florida, calling my business partner, calling my significant other, calling my mentor, praying for myself and the people in my life that I want to pray for. So I stop and ask, "What does sanity look like? How do I take care of myself when there are too many directions to go in at the same time—when there's too much adrenaline flowing?"

First, I try to meditate, but my mind is still racing. Trying to function with a racing mind is, for me, like being in a car whose driver is hell-bent to get nowhere fast and have a wreck on the way. And so I ask, "what am I powerless over right now?" I am powerless over all the tasks I think I need to do, like starting to move the contents of this five-bedroom house. I've already made a sane plan for this job—break it up into small pieces, a room at a time. Take only what we need for this interim in the small condo we're moving to, and store the rest.

Helping the movers now, with this compulsiveness, looks like a setup for a trashed back and being totally worn out by lunchtime. Then there are other to-do options to add to the list: clean out closets, pay bills, advertise the garage sale. Go. Go. Go. I cannot control this heart of mine that beats so fast sometimes when the compulsion is to get up and get started on my day before I get centered.

Starting my day before I am centered and focused means I am not nearly as likely to stay rational when it comes to spending, working, and saying no when someone asks me to do something I'd really rather not do. Starting this day not centered has disaster written all over it.

So I ask again, "What does sanity look like?" It looks like me sitting down to acknowledge my feelings of sadness (leaving this house with the great woods) and joy (leaving the debt), and to acknowledge my feelings that can come out as compulsiveness, urgency, anxiety, and hyperactivity. Sanity looks like accepting those feelings, breathing through them—breathing out the compulsiveness, breathing in the sanity—and being still. The deep breathing starts the process of peace in my body.

A little later I ask, "What does the insanity cost me?" It costs me my health and my serenity. It used to cost me money, because going out—to shop, to dinner, to pick up a few things at the grocery store—was a great distraction. When I left home in a rush to spend, I didn't create calm, productive days taking care of myself and my family. I constantly ran out of money, ran short before payday.

I stop, step back and without the emotion, visualize a sane and ordered day that ends with my being in bed at a decent hour, fed and clean, peaceful, and ready to turn my mind and body over to healing and restful sleep. If I, as Stephen Covey's second habit of highly successful people says, "begin with the end in mind," things are far more likely to move forward sanely. After all, we live the process and the results.

That said, I actually do feel calmer, like a sane, centered, rational adult, ready to put first things first and to have a day that may or may not be productive by my old workaholic standards. But however it is, it will be just fine by my standard for this moment: good and good enough.

THE TURNAROUND:

Mount Washmore Says Slow Down

The hours speed by faster than Christmas displays pop up on Halloween night. Faster than children, cranked up by the holidays, fire off lists of what they want from Santa. Even faster than laundry piles up after a weekend of being out of town.

For me, dirty laundry piled higher than two feet continues to be among the top three Overwhelm Indicators on my Personal Craziness Index (PCI) (acknowledgment to author Patrick Carnes, creator of the index, which appears in his wonderful book *A Gentle Path Through the Twelve Steps*).

My PCI is the chart I keep that tells me when I absolutely must stop everything I'm doing, be still, and figure out where to cut some activities out of my life, so I am doing the *one best* thing with my time, instead of scattering myself, my time, and my resources by trying to do *several very good* things.

Trimming the calendar—getting and keeping my priorities straight—is especially important with the advent of the holidays. At this time of the year, when emotional land mines prompt me to spend more, commit to more, eat more, and rush more, I have to be sure I have the time to handle the little everyday things that can seem explosive anytime, and absolutely nuclear at holiday time.

For example, on Tuesday morning I have no underwear for my four-year-old daughter. Where are all those Skivvies? I don't know. Two weeks ago, we were practically knee deep in Dalmatians, Pooh Bears, and Cinderellas—all stacked semineatly in her top drawer, waiting to be chosen.

A church retreat, a trip to Grandma's, a trip to my son's godparents, and a mountain of laundry later, clean Skivvies are scarce. And my seven-year-old will be late for first grade—a day breaker for sure—if I don't find something soon that will work for Sophie.

I head downstairs to the dryer, praying that dry, toasty-warm panties are part of the tumbling jumble inside. No such luck. So it comes down to this: "Sophie, you have a choice. You can wear the ones that are a little tight or the ones that are a little damp."

She chooses tight. I breathe a sigh of relief and hop on down the bunny trail toward getting everyone to school. Later, I can come back home and, in between calls, tackle Mount Washmore, polish up some work that's due to a client, and unload the dishwasher, so I can fill it again and finally see that shiny, elusive thing that's the bottom of my stainless steel sink.

This is where the rubber meets the road. It is time to go home. And stay home. It's time to wash more. And rush less. I am paying the price for the last three weekends away. And my children, who have very little choice in the matter, are paying, too.

Weekend Number One: Yes! We had fun on our church retreat.

Weekend Number Two: Absolutely! We needed to go be with my mother, to see how she is coping with her sudden bout of vertigo.

Weekend Number Three: No doubt about it! The trip to Kenny's godparents had been on the calendar for months. We couldn't reschedule that.

Well, we could have skipped or rescheduled two of those "necessities." And I probably could have endured saying no, at the risk of disappointing my children. The truth is, I must say no to so much activity because I am an exhaustible resource. And I am pretty much flying solo with all the responsibility—and opportunity—at hand.

So once again, I get the clear message. It is time to slow down. Get that reserve of size four Skivvies in the drawer. And spend some quiet, at-home family time with the precious wearer of that underwear, to show her, and her big brother, that at any time, but especially in the busy holiday time, our own little family is the best company of all.

The bottom line? I promise to slow down. I know how to do it, but I must practice slowing down with the little things, and the big things, every day. Especially now, because right now I *can* choose to slow down. But if I start running from one meeting to the next—one weekend activity or party to the next—I'll slam into a speed bump called trouble and be slowed down for sure. Or we'll be stopped by a hurting child who has to go to the pediatrician's office for the earache brought on by the cold brought on by getting run down, or by me getting slammed with bronchitis or a stiff neck, or by me—God forbid—falling asleep at the wheel.

Thank God, this time the signal to slow down is brought on *before* the holiday madness by a healthy but tired four-year-old sitting in the middle of her bedroom floor saying, "Mommy, I need some underwear."

The phone rings, trying to catch us as we leave. I ignore it. We get to school on time. And I'm the one who's learned the most important lesson: peace on Earth and God's abundance begin right here at the foot of a pile of dirty laundry.

Sane Ways to Manage Time Equals No Rushing

৩৯৯

1. *Your car is not the place to make up time if you're running late.* No matter how late you are or how important the event is that you're trying to get to, nothing is worth speeding and taking the risk of having an accident. Plan your day so that the time in your car isn't rushed. (We're trying to eliminate *any* rushing.) Driving under the influence of rush and the resulting excess adrenaline is extremely dangerous. Remember what a serious undertaking it is to drive with children in your car, and that your children need to be alive more than they need to be "on time."

2. *No matter how rushed or desperate you are, never get into the car with someone who has been drinking or is acting out emotionally, or let your children ride with someone who has been drinking, is too tired to drive, or is in an agitated, emotional state.* Certainly do not

drink and drive yourself. TurnAround Parents don't
let children get into the car with anyone who is drinking, rushing, or acting irrationally. The risk far out-
weighs any possible benefit.

3. ***TurnAround Parents get up a little earlier than necessary to have a reserve of time, just in case.*** Rushing is
a sign that we are trying to do too much. The solution
is to reprioritize, prepare better, or simply do less. You
can't really manage time, but you can manage yourself. It also helps to remember the "Rule of One or
Two," taught to me by a wise mom who said it's best
not to try to fit more than one or two major events into
a child's day. For example, a Saturday morning birthday party and running a few errands is okay. A morning party, errands, and an afternoon soccer game can
set a child up for a meltdown. Children need time to
transition from one activity/location to the next. And
they need lots of unstructured, hanging out "downtime" at home, just being with their parent(s), even if
part of that time is spent doing family chores.

4. ***Children who are rushed will act out their frustration eventually.*** It is abusive to constantly rush children. It makes them think something is wrong with them, that they can never go fast enough or keep up.

5. ***Budget time to allow for your children's pace.*** You will all be happier. It also helps to have children get up fifteen minutes earlier than usual. Just try it, and see if this reserve of time doesn't help your morning go more smoothly by allowing the children to move more at their own pace. When you leave fifteen minutes earlier than necessary for school, work, and everything else, you'll be less stressed.

6. ***Let your children be responsible for waking themselves up with their own alarm clocks.*** This encourages responsibility and makes them more aware of time.

7. ***Do your grocery shopping alone if possible.*** You'll get out of the store faster, spend less, and probably come home with healthier foods.

8. *Have the children prepare for the next day by laying out their clothes on their beds and putting their shoes by the door; do the same with book bags and snacks.* Pack them before bed. Make all of this a part of your nightly routine. You won't waste time looking for clothes, shoes, or homework the next morning.

9. *Post a morning and evening schedule, and stick to it.* This structure helps you every bit as much as it does your children. Sticking to schedules, rules, and consequences is one of the best ways to avoid blowups because children need and respond well to consistency.

10. *When you first get home, take a few minutes to connect with your children before you start to cook dinner or help with homework.* Sit on the sofa with them for just five or ten minutes listening to them talk about their day or reading to them. Once they've connected with you, they'll go play on their own instead of fighting and vying for your attention in negative ways, saving you time and frustration later.

10

Honor Your Family's Future

There are few comforts in the world like that of sitting with your children, drinking hot chocolate, and eating popcorn while they get their homework done and you do your own homework (balance your checkbook, pay bills, write notes, clip grocery coupons, and so on). It is a holy time. Treat it as such. Give your children the space, time, peace, and quiet to do their work, and they will perform better than you could ever imagine. Make school the priority before all the extracurricular activities, and they will learn how to set priorities.

Be a lifelong student yourself. Find something you want to study, and let them see you excited about studying; it will help them be excited about their schoolwork. Foster a love of learning by reading to your children and having them read to you, even road signs and cereal boxes. It pays to create an environment where you're always learning something, where there's respect for education and self-improvement.

THE PAIN STARTS HERE:

acid rock and my homework

It must be about 9:00 PM. I have a book to finish reading, a report to write, and God only knows what else. I've had a bath and am ready to settle down and get this homework finished, when the electric guitar on the other side of my bedroom wall cranks up, and suddenly I'm drowning in my eleven-year-old brother's butchering of Jimi Hendrix's "Purple Haze."

He's got the stereo on, too, trying to play along with Jimi, as I try desperately to concentrate. But it just doesn't work. It takes me forever to settle down to get going on the assignments. And then I need some peace and quiet. I beg Mother to do something about the noise. The kid has had all afternoon to play that thing. It's nighttime—time for me to get my homework done.

Mother is on the phone. She's always on the phone, confirming her appointments for the next day and talking to her friends. "I'll be finished in a minute." It's 9:20.

Fifteen minutes later I'm ready to scream. She's finally off the phone. I'm in my brother's room threatening to break that damned electric guitar into a thousand pieces if he doesn't shut it off. She says she'll make him turn it down. She's laughing about how angry I am. I could kill her, too. I hate it when she does that. I feel angry and like crying at the same time. She always sides with him because he's younger, and she feels sorry for him. I go back to work.

Five minutes later the little bastard has cranked the volume back up again, and Mother is back on the phone. I want to kill him. I really do. I need to study. I am so behind. I'm always behind. Band practice ran late. By the time I ate supper and showered, it was 8:30. It took me thirty minutes just to organize all the stuff I have to do. Then, "Nair, nair, nair . . . nair, nair, nair, nair . . . Purple haze, gets in my eyes, . . ." Excuse me while I want to die.

Mother and I go back and forth arguing until about 10:00 PM, when it's time for my brother to go to bed. I've tried everything. Cotton in my ears. Doors closed. Towels around my head. Putting my head in the hair dryer with the hair dryer on. Nothing blocks out the cheap-ass guitar and the big-ass amplifier he got for his birthday. He manages to annoy me for a while longer until Mother makes him go to bed. I have a few minutes of peace and quiet until Daddy gets home.

My brother sleeps through it. He always does. But not me. I hear them in the kitchen, Mother and Daddy fighting like crazy. She's trying to put some supper on the table for him. He wants his canned tomato, oyster, saltine cracker, canned sardine stew slop that he craves when he's drunk. I feel sick just thinking about it.

Mother walks on eggshells for about forty more minutes until she can get Daddy to bed. I sit on eggshells the whole time, zoning in and out of the homework that's due, waiting for there to be some explosion in the kitchen. Finally, I fall asleep on my notebook, drooling all over the report I'm working on. When I wake up I've got spiral notebook marks on my face. Great.

About 11:15 Mother comes in and asks me if I am finished. I say no, but that I'll get up early and work in the morning. I crawl into bed and read for a little while. Then I sleep and wake up a bunch of times until it's time to get up. God knows I don't want to get out of bed. I'll do anything not to have to face the day. Then I hear that electric guitar again—a little of the group Iron Butterfly's "In-A-Gadda-Da-Vida" before we leave for school. Hell's bells. I just throw everything in my book bag and trudge into the kitchen to leave for school. I am worn out and not finished with my homework—again. I am scared to go into class without it, frustrated, and ready to give up on school. For about the millionth time, I wish I were dead.

History Almost Repeats Itself:
The Car Pool Line

It is the end of my workday and time to go and pick up my children. I wonder what lies ahead. With my eight-year-old son, who's hurting because his father isn't coming to visit as planned, there may be intense anger. Whether it's directed at his father or not, my son's anger rains down around me in his unwillingness to eat supper, bathe, or complete homework.

My vague sense of dread is almost like it was when I was a little girl wondering how my angry, alcoholic father would be when he got home. Happy? Raging? Loving? Normal?

The difference is that, of course, now I am a mature TurnAround Mom who's been through dozens of self-help and parenting workshops and years of therapy to learn patience, consciousness, and assertiveness, so I can be strong and centered when this kid gets in the car and acts like he could chew the heads off of his sister's My Little Ponies and destroy half the free world before supper.

Though I do think about screaming sometimes, I am truly able, from a centered and loving state, to take whatever my son dishes out and be strong and in authority and not let his anger throw me off my path of being a loving single mother who is there for him, no matter what. (His precious sister has her moments of alien possession as well, but is in a pretty decent mood right now, since we're reading her favorite book this week, and she got that pink suede cowgirl outfit with the fringe.)

Yes! I am present. So let them roar in traffic, scowl over my supper selection, and act out until their faces turn blue. I am their mother, and I know they need a boundaried place of unconditional love to let their dirty hair down and cut loose their sadness and disappointment.

Besides, I have the Game Boy held hostage. And Kenny knows that acting out after the third warning means no sleepover friend tomorrow night. You see, I'm into consequences because I am *the Mom in Charge*. My claim to authority is not about ego; it is about making sure there's a sane, reliable adult around to set limits, give encouragement, kiss boo-boos, and make sure there's some peace and quiet every day. Children like all of that. They need it. It makes them feel safe and secure, especially in the face of change or upset.

So I keep telling myself that I am the rock, that I won't react and yell back when they yell; the volume only gets louder and then nothing gets heard. Even if I'm tempted, I won't hit; it only makes children think it's okay to hit. Even though I have the most cutting comeback lines in the world, I won't be sarcastic, rude, or shaming.

Because with children, like computers, what you put in is what you get out. The quickest way to end a war with children is to disengage, redirect the focus, or simply go silent for a few minutes. De-escalate. Respond instead of react.

Even though there are moments when I am tempted to pitch my own hissy fit, go shopping, and give up on the work I need to do, with God's help I won't. I am a loving, sane mother who is, like all moms, challenged and tested. I am sometimes also toasted, roasted, fried, and tried. But I know what gives me strength. I know how to ask for help. I can take deep breaths and drive at the same time. In the ten-minute journey from my front door to the car pool line, I can go a million miles and back and end up in a sane, loving place. I love this little boy and see him, in this moment, for what he is: He is not a little boy who wants to hurt me. He is just a little boy who is hurting.

It seems I have finally learned the power of a quiet word, an act of praise, or biting my tongue when I know, deep down, that trying to reason with a hurting, volcanic child is as pointless as trying to put out fires with napalm. Even if being calm doesn't work, it goes a lot farther than arguing or criticizing.

I can only guess at what kind of emotional shape my eight-year-old is in. But I do know where I'm coming from. And as long as I'm coming from sanity and love, I can't go wrong.

The Two-Handkerchief Graduation

I t's a quick flashback at my son's fifth-grade graduation. As I look for an open chair, I remember taking
my seat at one of the most important meetings of
my life: a meeting with the principal at this wonderful
elementary school where my freckle-faced little boy has
grown into a handsome young man.

Tonight the fifth-graders line up for the hour cere-
mony, and I relive how much I felt like a little girl myself
that day back in 1995, when trying to be businesslike, I
waited to see the principal. As Mrs. Young introduced
herself to me, I was so overwhelmed with fear and emotion I could barely swallow the knot in the top of my
throat. My hands never stopped shaking the whole time
I was there.

Why was I so fragile? I'd been divorced about a year
and had an emotional six-year-old son and his baby sister to care for. I was looking for stability and comfort
from every healthy source possible. We'd missed the

zoning cut to be in this school district by less than a mile; I needed an administrative transfer. I thought that if the principal said yes to my request for a transfer, my son would be in the best school possible for him. After all, most of his prekindergarten buddies would be here. And I believed he'd be much happier if he didn't have to go through the stress of getting used to a new group of kids.

If he got into this elementary school it would also be a tremendous help to me. Kenny would have easy access to the after-school program at the same place where he'd been in prekindergarten; he could ride the bus over with his classmates and see familiar teachers. I wouldn't have to leave work in the middle of the day to deal with taking him somewhere else through major traffic, as I might if he went to school in our assigned school district. Further, he'd be right across the street from Sophie, making afternoon pickups a snap.

I remembered how Mrs. Young came in and sat down across from me. Cool. Collected. Professional. I was waif-like at the time, still a jangle of nerves, with all the fight of a mother tiger ready to die to provide for her young.

My objective was to get a yes answer and leave her office before dissolving into a puddle of stress-induced sobs. She listened patiently, giving me time to catch my breath and wipe my eyes as needed. At one point, her eyes looked moist.

As it turned out, she couldn't give me the answer; it had to come from higher up in the school system. But she would be able to approve or disapprove their transfer recommendation. And the pointers she gave me were simple and valuable. She said, "Write what you've told me today in a letter—just the way you said it here. Be the first in line on the morning you can apply for the transfer." In earlier times I might have tried to pull some strings: get in touch with people I knew at the mayor's office or something like that. But those days were over. The truth would have to work, or not. Beyond that, I knew I needed to pray. And turn this request for help over to God.

My remembering all of this is interrupted by "Pomp and Circumstance" and seeing those eighty-plus faces I've watched mature from cherubic five-year-olds to snaggle-toothed second-graders to charming young ladies and gentlemen. My son walks in, escorting one of the special-needs children. I am filled with joy and with memories of the relief I felt when I knew we had the administrative transfer and Mrs. Young's approval. The transfer had come just days before Kenny was to start kindergarten; Mrs. Young's approval came as soon as she received her copy of the school board's transfer.

What a time we'd had at this school/home, starting out with an amazing kindergarten teacher who was queen of her own jungle. Her room was filled with hopping, creeping, slithering things that delighted my children and me. One long holiday weekend I even took home her favorite creature, Ratigran, the rat.

Through the years, Mrs. Young became Carole. She always seemed to be in the hallway as I crept in with a forgotten lunch, brought Kenny from taking his allergy shots, or just came by to peek in and see what was going on when I was having one of my world's-most-paranoid-mom days. Sometimes she and I would chat for a minute or two.

When it came time to see if Sophie could get the administrative transfer, too, Carole's good advice worked a second time.

Again my reminiscing is interrupted, this time by the first of the delightful speeches being delivered by the graduating fifth-graders. Each child speaks for about thirty seconds about his or her best memory at school.

Sweet voices sing touching songs between each group of speeches. I go back into my reverie for a few minutes, remembering other conversations with Carole. She's been gone from the school for a year now. It was incredible to think that she would ever leave, but she did, after dozens of years, because she didn't want to wait until she was "totally burned out." I admired her leaving on an up note.

As the teacher in charge of the graduation program finishes her speech, she tells us there's a surprise guest of honor. Everyone in the auditorium stands, and the applause is thunderous as Mrs. Young takes the podium to say a few words to the graduating class she served for five of their six years.

She is eloquent, as always. I am moved to tears by her being there, by the videotaped collection of memories a mom has put to music and duplicated for each child, by the singing of the school spirit song, and by my son's walking past me, out of grammar school, into the rest of his life.

Later, I see Carole, and she gives me a hug. Our eyes fill with tears as I thank her for meeting with me six years earlier. I believe she's taken a special interest over the years in how well Kenny has done. Without her help, he might not have been in this incredibly wonderful little school. At the same time, in view of all that Carole knows about me, my past, my challenges, it feels terrific when she tells me she knows we've come a long way since I was that scared-to-death single mom in her office so long ago. And that she's proud of all of us.

And so we have come full circle, starting and ending Kenny's time here with Mrs. Young's blessing. Kenny may have been the one graduating, but for me—knowing that I have fostered a love of learning in him and his sister, got him to school with lunch and homework more than 1,100 days, and earned the respect of an educator I'll always admire—it felt as though I had graduated more than honorably as well.

❧

Sane Ways to
Honor Your Family's Future

❦

1. *View your children's school as a great support to your own growth and turnaround.* It is a source of structure and discipline in your life and theirs. Have a good attitude about school. It will help them have a good attitude about it, too.

2. *Show your children that schoolwork is important by making time for homework in the evening and by getting them to school early.*

3. *Pick up your children from school and after-school activities on time.* It helps them to feel secure and important. Nobody likes being the last person to be picked up.

4. *Build time into your day to avoid rushing anywhere, but especially to school.* Also, start their day off right. No arguing on the way to school, no matter what.

5. **ESPECIALLY FOR SINGLE, WORKING MOMS:** *If your children are in an after-school program and can do homework there with the help of a teacher, encourage them to do so.* If they do homework at home and need your help, fine. But the more you can avoid being the "police" for everything—homework, room clean-up, bath—the better. This doesn't mean you are shirking your responsibility. The reality is that it is virtually impossible to do it all, and it's okay to ask for help.

6. *Tell your child's new teachers how your children operate:* "My son needs lots of eye contact and must be in the front of the room." "My daughter responds well to hearing her name; she has a vision problem and does best when she's close to the board."

7. **ESPECIALLY IMPORTANT TO SINGLE MOMS:** *Your children need to be around strong, moral men who revere learning and are role models for accountability.* You will find these men teaching Sunday school, chaperoning youth groups at the temple, coaching at the local Y, being Big Brothers, volunteering at Boys &

Girls Clubs of America. They are the fathers of the friends your children meet at church, synagogue, temple, wherever it is that you go to worship and give thanks. Put your children in the Sunday school, temple, and sports programs that give them opportunities to know and be guided by good, moral, responsible men.

8. *Get outdoors and exercise with your children.* Teach them the value of taking a walk, raking leaves, getting outside for fresh air and exercise. People in the United States need to eat less and exercise more. Obesity and lack of exercise are leading causes of illness and premature death.

9. *Have your own nightly reading/study/quiet time to delve into materials important to your personal growth.* Have your children read while you read. Your example shows them that studying is important to you, too. It's also a great prelude to reading and praying together at the end of the day.

10. ***Children thrive on praise.*** Help your children succeed by giving them gentle encouragement. Make statements that let them know you believe in their competence by recalling something specific they've done well.

11. ***Have books available at home—your own or those you borrow from the library.*** It's valuable for children to always have access to good reading material, even in the car. Also, provide materials at home for creative activity—construction paper, water-based markers and paints, glue, puzzles, and board games—rather than relying on television or electronic games.

12. ***Read to your children daily and invite them to read to you.*** This time close together strengthens your bond with your children, fosters a love of learning, and is a memory your children will treasure.

11

Next Steps

As I sit here finishing this book, my life seems to hang in balance. My ex-husband, who has been just two hours away for the last two years, is living a thousand miles away again. For a while I had come to count on the children being with him and his wife one or two weekends a month. That had been valuable time for them to reconnect with their dad, which I've definitely encouraged, and it had been downtime, recovery time, catch-up time for me. And now it looks as though the children will see him only once or twice a year.

And that's where being a TurnAround Mom really comes into play for me. Because I have to literally "let go and let God." Sure, I could try to control the situation (old tape playing) and ask their dad to stay closer to us in terms of geography, as I've done several times before. Yet no matter where he's lived, he has always done his best to let the children know he loves and cares for them. It's not in anyone's best interest for me to complain about his moving. In our divorce agreement, we swore never to say anything negative about each other to the children. I won't start now. I'll just pray for God's will in all of this and know that I have the support, the sanity, or whatever it is that I need, right here, right now, by asking for God's help and reaching out to my support network.

Who knows? I might even find that it's God's will for me to pick up and head west, too. And if that's what God wants, I'm willing, though I don't want to leave my family and friends.

And I don't need to get that far ahead of myself. I need to stay in this moment, enjoying the simple pleasures of life and parenting, one day at a time.

THE TURNAROUND:

Blessed Be the Tide That Binds

As I wrote when I started my own turnaround almost twelve years ago:

*I*t is a little after midnight. I am sorting my way through a three-foot-high pile of laundry on my bed. I am in that dog-tired mother-fog, when I have a sudden epiphany. I see what is holy in doing laundry.

In folding those little clothes, I feel the soft cotton that guards the precious skin on my children's wondrous little bodies. I see the hand-me-downs that go from one to the other. The designs of fish or lions or turtles or tigers woven into the fabric of the shirt I am touching bring to life memories that are woven together to protect our souls, our minds, our hearts and give a design—a pattern—to our lives.

For so long I have thought myself above doing laundry. I tell myself I have better things to do. It is not the highest and best use of my valuable time and talents. Hrrumph.

But now I see how I have shortchanged myself for not being fully present in this process. How I have missed—or almost missed—a simple pleasure. The simple pleasure of giving them a blank slate—a clean shirt—on which to keep a diary of their days, written in mustard and blackberry jam and Bosco. I find joy in these stains. They tell stories I am not always around to hear.

Not meaning to romanticize material things, mind you, but I suddenly see how in tending to that which touches and protects my loved ones—even the humblest catsup-stained T-shirt—I care for my loved ones.

This is a functional thing to do. It is honest, and it is honorable. And I am grateful—so grateful—for the opportunity to do it. To have these soon-to-be-outgrown jeans to patch for the little sister. She is Grace. This is grace.

Of course, keeping my children in clean clothes is a small part of the big picture. The big picture that I pray they will step away from years from now and say, "She might not have always remembered every party, every practice, every PTA meeting, but she sure loved us. She asked us how we were feeling, she cared enough to make consequences stick, and she helped us live our dreams."

And so, as they sleep and I fold, sort, cleanse, and mend, I thank God for one more small way to stay in touch with *them. It's something I haven't always done very well in the past. And now I'm doing it.*

Enough. It's time to put the final rinse on this rambling about the holiness of laundry and say, "This is the laundry day the Lord has made. I will rejoice and be glad in it."

Blessed be the Tide that binds!

Every day is a gift. If life brings me lemons, I can twist up my mouth and refuse to appreciate their wake-me-up flavor, or I can search out a little sweetness and make lemonade. I can sink into "poor me" mode, or I can sit down and write out my gratitude list for the zillionth time.

Things seem to work best when I stop trying to interpret events or to label them as good or bad. The circumstances are what they are; reading something good or bad into them is a waste of energy. The best action I can take is to simply deal with life on life's terms. From a sane and loving place, I can stay out of interpretation and just live and let be.

The only predictable thing about life is change. Change keeps us alive. And life is good, even if, under the microscope of the moment, it may seem bad.

Yes, like everybody else, I get tired. And I know there are many single parents whose partners have never been around. Furthermore, I recognize that thousands of them—thousands of *us*—rise above feeling overwhelmed and do an incredibly terrific job of rearing responsible, productive, wonderful children.

So, I will pray. And I will read my own book. As I said, I wrote this book for me as much as I did for anyone. Because there really is no conclusion here, thank God. The job of a TurnAround Parent never really ends. As long as we are around children—not just our own, but any child—we have the opportunity to help create a saner, more loving world for them and ourselves, by remembering and acting on these truths:

You are a blessing,
and I'm glad you're here.

To help raise you,
I must first raise myself.

When I visit with women at the treatment centers, they are always overjoyed to hear that I must have learned something from my chapter on relationships, since, after being a single mom for eleven years, I married a truly wonderful man who is a loving husband and stepfather.

The gifts of recovery are terrific blessings in a new marriage. Acceptance, gratitude, patience—all the qualities we learn as we gain greater compassion for ourselves—are invaluable tools in forging new family relationships.

Resources

❧❧❧

For Your Own TurnAround

Al-Anon, 1-800-425-2666, www.al-anon.org

Alcoholics Anonymous (A.A.), check your local telephone directory, or visit the website www.aa.org

Childhelp, 24-hour hotline 1-800-422-4453 (TDD 1-800-222-4453), www.childhelpusa.org

Children and Adults with Attention Deficit/Hyperactivity Disorder (CHADD), 1-800-233-4050, www.chadd.org

Debtors Anonymous, 888-554-COAS (2627), 781-453-2743, www.debtorsanonymous.org

National Association for Children of Alcoholics, 301-468-0987, www.nacoa.net

National Domestic Violence Hotline, 1-800-799-SAFE (7233), (TDD 1-800-787-3224), www.ndvh.org

National Organization on Fetal Alcohol Syndrome, 202-785-4585, www.nofas.org

Overeaters Anonymous, 505-891-2664, www.oa.org

Prevent Child Abuse America, 312-663-3520,
www.preventchildabuse.org

Sex Addicts Anonymous, 1-800-477-8191 (USA and
Canada), 1-713-869-4902 (all other countries),
www.sexaa.org

Recommended Reading

Adult Children of Alcoholics by Janet Woititz

Boundaries with Kids by Henry Cloud and John Townsend

Breaking Free: A Recovery Workbook for Facing Codependence by Pia Mellody and Andrea Wells Miller

Codependent No More by Melody Beattie

A Gentle Path Through the Twelve Steps by Patrick Carnes

How to Get Out of Debt, Stay Out of Debt, and Live Prosperously by Jerrold Mundis

It Will Never Happen to Me by Claudia Black

Money Drunk, Money Sober by Julia Cameron and Mark Bryan

The 7 Habits of Highly Effective Families by Stephen R. Covey

The Verbally Abusive Relationship by Patricia Evans

Notes

Chapter Two

1. When I was much older I learned that my grandpa abused my sweet little grandma and beat the snot out of my angel-faced daddy when he was a boy. Grandma had nowhere to turn for help. Rural Georgia had no shelters for battered women back then; some places still don't. There weren't any in the 1960s, either, when Mother and my brother and I needed a safe place, when nobody wanted anyone to know about Daddy's problem. We'd rather die looking good than run the risk of letting anyone know his dark secrets: that the "Santa Claus" with those cotton balls glued to his navy photo had jumped on the back of a chicken truck at the age of fifteen and ridden it from North Georgia to South Florida because he was scared to death of his own father's rage and thought he had no one to turn to but an alcoholic stepbrother in Miami; that he had lied about his age so he could join the navy, where he was a great boxer, saw his

best friend's head blown off, and drank too much; that he came home, married my mother, and became as violent as his father ever was.

He could fight a war, build businesses, kill big deer, and make hundreds of thousands of dollars, but just like his father before him, my daddy couldn't ask for or accept help when it came to figuring out a way to stop hurting himself and the people he loved most.

Chapter Eight

1. Mother and I didn't talk about Daddy's shooting at us for more than thirty years. She'd put it out of her mind. I was able to remember it only about ten years ago.

It's amazing how being around alcoholism makes it easy to stay loyal to people who do deadly, illegal, immoral, and demonic things. It's amazing how being around alcoholism, addiction, abuse, and toxic intensity can make you stuff down even the most horrifying experiences. We gloss them over and put a parking lot on top of the volcano.

But crazy experiences with an alcoholic don't just get glossed over, really. Those memories, however repressed, go into the mix as fuel for more toxic intensity. They keep coming out, generation after generation, until finally we open the wounds and clean them by talking about what happened—maybe even screaming about it, crying about it, beating pillows about it again and again—until, even though we can never forget it, we can forgive it, and hopefully go on to nurture ourselves and stay clean and clear about the things that happen in the present.

2. Today I wonder why therapists I saw over the years didn't recommend Alcoholics Anonymous or Al-Anon to me. I believe thousands of mental health professionals, pastoral counselors included, gloss over or fail to recognize their clients' addictions and co-addictions, missing the opportunity to send clients and their families to the twelve-step programs that can save lives and help prevent years of self-destruction and misery.

Amazing TurnAround Moms
and a Request for Your Story!

※

I n my work with women at recovery centers and other organizations, I've come to know some amazing mothers who are the epitome of TurnAround Moms.

They are women in recovery from addiction and abuse. They are women with mental illness and developmental disabilities. They are women who are trying desperately to turn their lives around and make life better for their children.

Some are survivors of an abuse that happened before they were even born: their mothers drank alcohol while they were pregnant, resulting in their being born with a severe degree of fetal alcohol spectrum disorder.

Some of the mothers in recovery fear that their own children have been damaged by their drinking and drug abuse while pregnant. They are in so much pain, fearing or knowing that they've caused irreversible damage to their children. They are learning that to make life better for their children, they must stay sober and create stability and consistency, routine and order.

Most of the women in the different support groups I see are strong women of great faith. They are girlfriends or wives or ex-wives who are survivors of unimaginable horrors dealt to them by parents, neighbors, friends, strangers, lovers, or husbands. In one group of women I know, most of the women were raped before they were twelve years old.

And yet every other week I see them coming in for their support group, showing up and asking for help. Listening to each other and learning to trust; talking with each other and wanting to be a support to other women.

They are inspiring. They are among the millions of TurnAround Moms I celebrate each day.

In this book I've told you about my ongoing efforts to be a TurnAround Mom. In my next book I would like to tell you about other moms who are turning their lives around, making life better for themselves and their children.

If you are a TurnAround Mom and would like to send

your story to me for possible inclusion in a book or another celebration of mothers, please visit me at www. turnaroundmom.com. Your story can be anonymous.

My dream is to find innovative, tangible ways to support mothers who are trying to make life better for themselves and their children. As I continue my work to support mothers, my prayers and good wishes go out for every mom who wants the best for her children. I look forward to hearing from you soon.

—Carey

About the Author

❧

Carey Sipp, the dynamic author of *The TurnAround Mom*, is an addiction and abuse survivor and parenting education advocate. To stop the heartbreaking cycles of addiction and abuse destroying our families, she believes Americans must break our collective addiction to what she calls toxic intensity, "the mother of all addictions."

A single mom for eleven years, Carey was married in 2005 and now has three stepchildren in addition to her teenage son and daughter.

For many years, Carey, a Georgia Author of the Year nominee, was an award-winning advertising creative director, primarily working on fundraising materials for nonprofit organizations, such as children's hospitals, children's causes, the arts, and educational institutions.

Carey is a writer, speaker, and inventor who is known for her honesty, sense of humor, and her ability to touch the hearts and minds of her audience.

A graduate of the University of Tennessee with a degree in communications, she is able to address topics including addiction, abuse, parenting, recovery, and children's needs. She is also a certified presenter/trainer for the Georgia Crisis Intervention Team, teaching crisis intervention and de-escalation skills to law enforcement officers. She is available as a speaker for civic groups, recovery centers, workshops, events, and conferences, and is working on her next book.

She may be reached at: **www.turnaroundmom.com**.